Mom's Homeschooling Handbook

Name: & Age:

Address:

Phone & Email:

TEACH By Example

Doodle

PLAY

PLAN

LEARN

CREATE

LOVE

Mom's Homeschooling Handbook

Copyright Information

This workbooks is for Home and Family use only. You may make copies of these materials for only the children in your household.

All other uses of this material must be permitted in writing by the Thinking Tree LLC. It is a violation of copyright law to distribute the electronic files or make copies for your friends, associates or students without our permission.

For information on using these materials for businesses, co-ops, summer camps, day camps, daycare, afterschool program, churches, or schools please contact us for licensing.

Contact Us:

The Thinking Tree LLC
617 N. Swope St. Greenfield, IN 46140. United States
317.622.8852 PHONE (Dial +1 outside of the USA) 267.712.7889 FAX

Do-It-Yourself Homeschooling
www.DyslexiaGames.com

jbrown@DyslexiaGames.com

INSTRUCTIONS

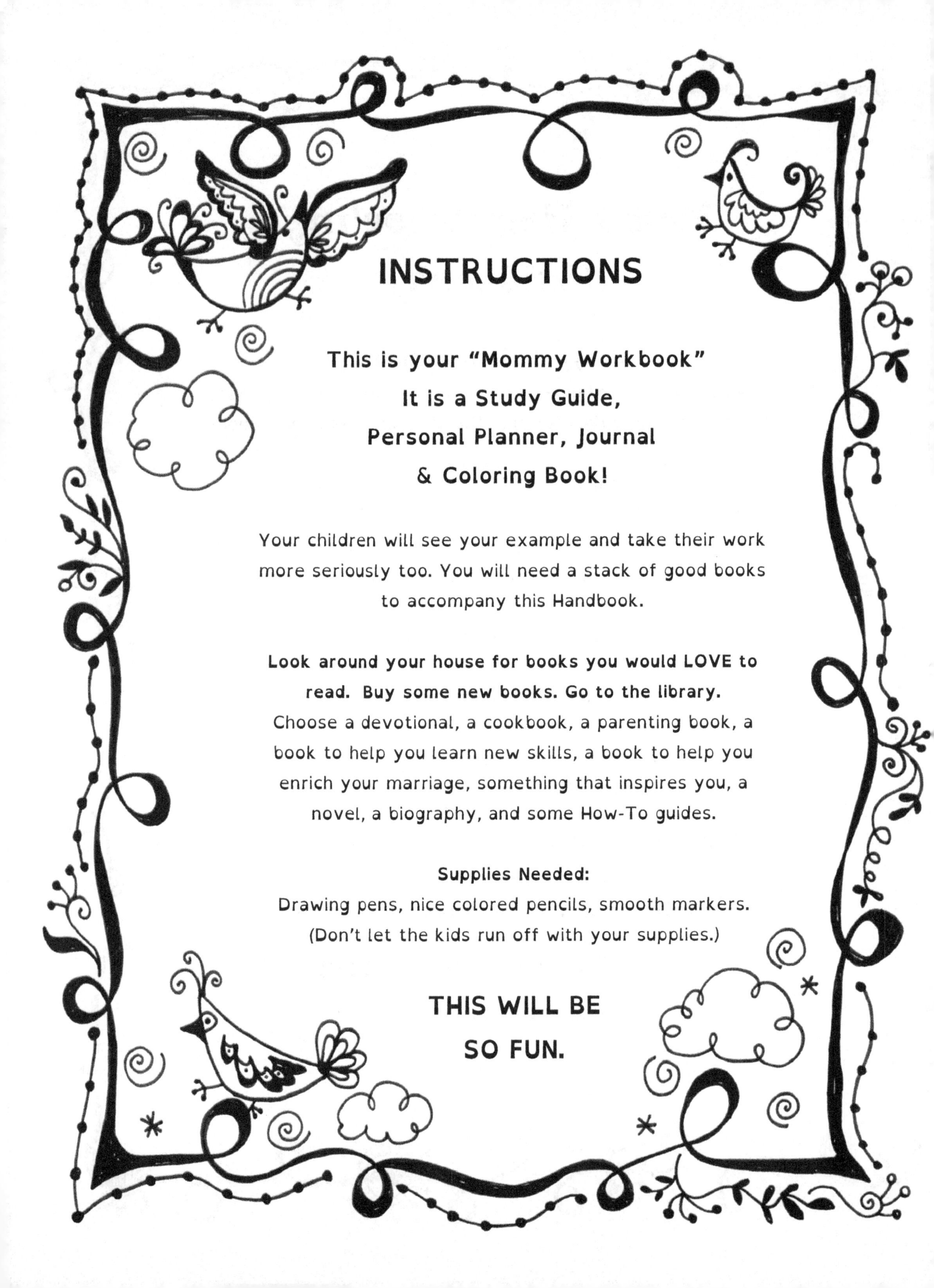

This is your "Mommy Workbook"
It is a Study Guide,
Personal Planner, Journal
& Coloring Book!

Your children will see your example and take their work more seriously too. You will need a stack of good books to accompany this Handbook.

Look around your house for books you would LOVE to read. Buy some new books. Go to the library.
Choose a devotional, a cookbook, a parenting book, a book to help you learn new skills, a book to help you enrich your marriage, something that inspires you, a novel, a biography, and some How-To guides.

Supplies Needed:
Drawing pens, nice colored pencils, smooth markers.
(Don't let the kids run off with your supplies.)

THIS WILL BE SO FUN.

Choose Nine Books To Read & Study!

1. Write down the titles on each cover below.
2. Keep your stack of books in a safe place.
3. Be ready to read a few pages from 3 or 4 of your books daily.
4. Complete a few pages each day in this Handbook.

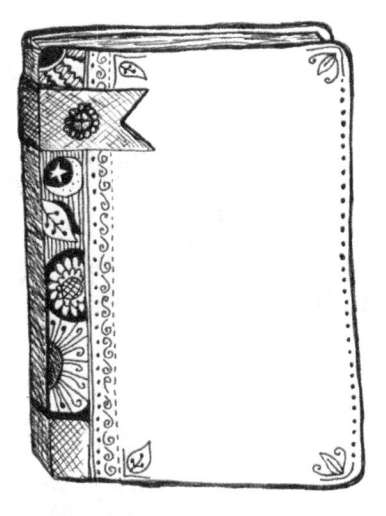

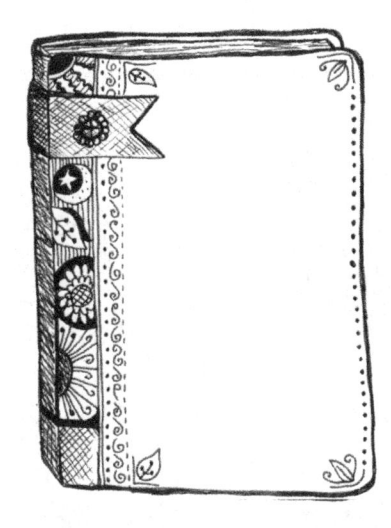

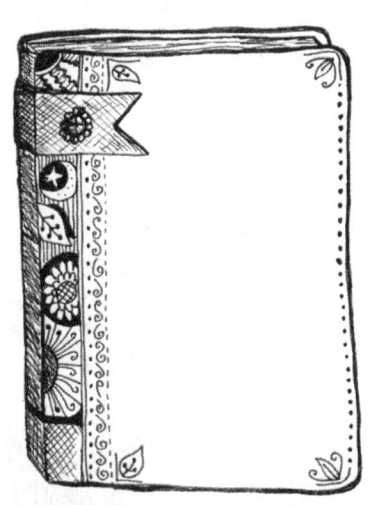

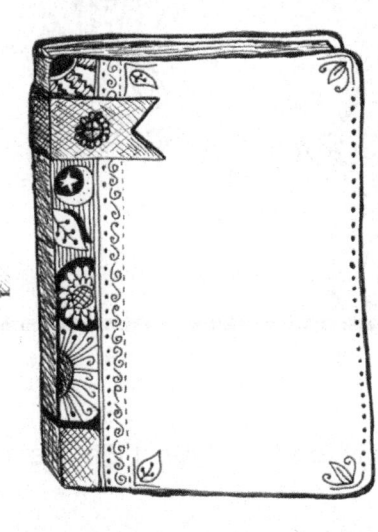

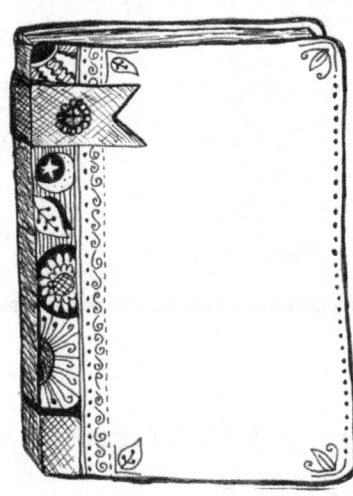

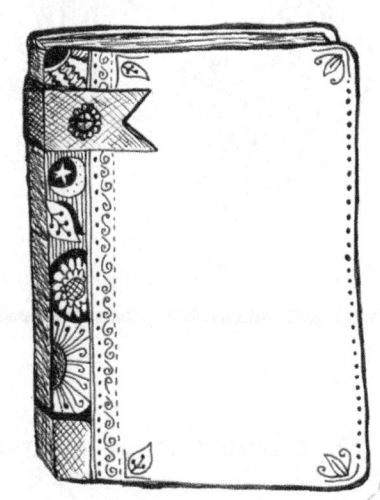

Mom's Coloring Time

Coloring beautiful pictures and doodling relieves stress and helps with creativity & relaxation.

"The true sign of intelligence is not knowledge but imagination." ~ Albert Einstein

A New Day!

My Verse, My Song or My Prayer...

What Matters Most...

Prayer List

Reading Time

Sit down with a few books from your stack.

Write, draw or copy the things you want to remember.

Plans & Perspective

"The home is the first and most effective place to learn the lessons of life: truth, honor, virtue, self control, the value of education, honest work, and the purpose and privilege of life." - McKay

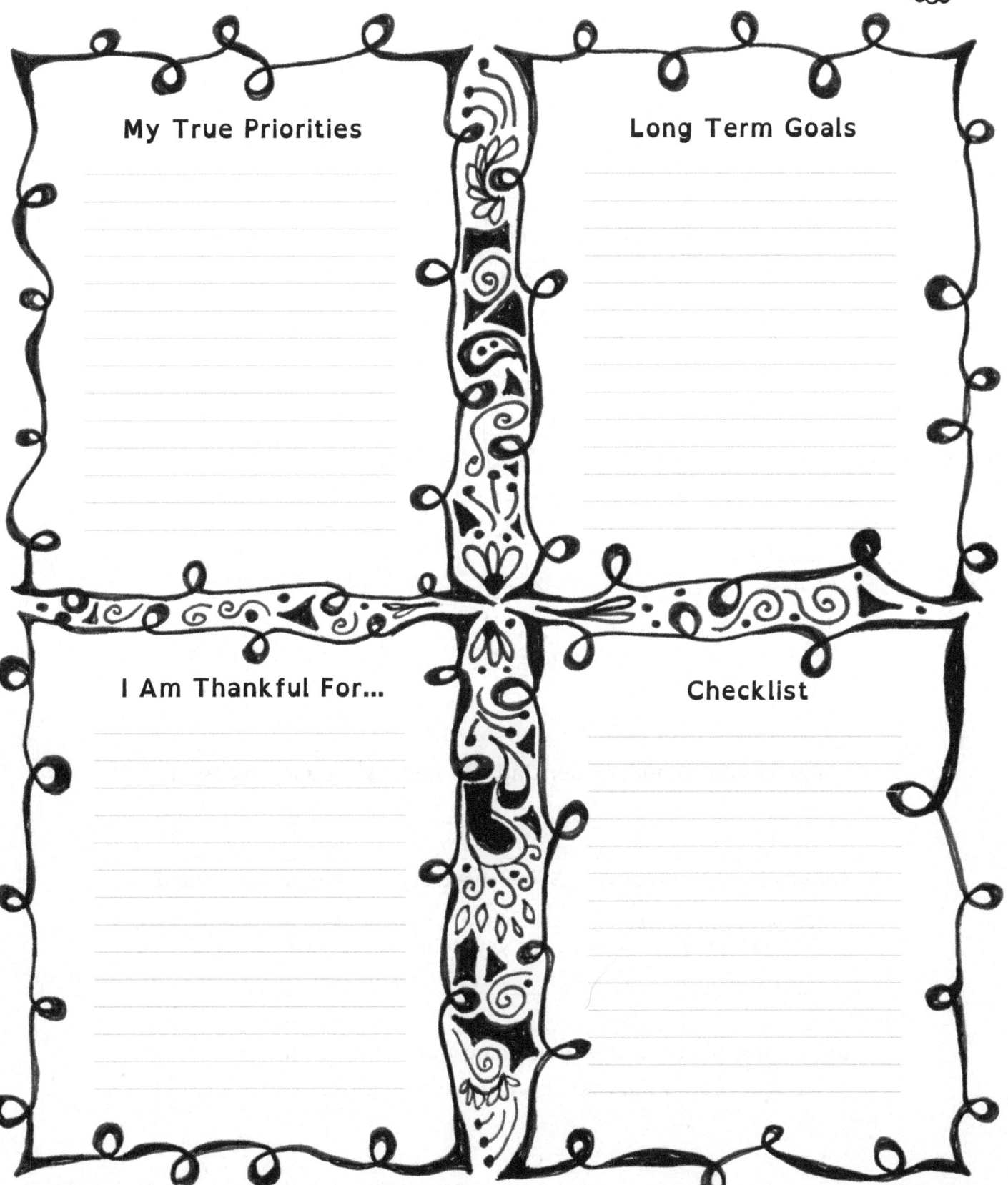

My True Priorities

Long Term Goals

I Am Thankful For...

Checklist

Attitude Improvement Time

How are your feeling today?
Color all the facial expressions that match your day!

happy	surprised	joy	doubt	distrust
self-sufficiency	dreamy	shocked	scared	guile
gloomy	engrossment	flash	determination	thoughtful
diffidence	offence	confusion	craft	tired

How is your mood influencing the people around you today?

_____
_____

Do you need a cup of tea? Some chocolate? A hug? A quiet moment?

Peaceful music? Stop the clock. Make it happen. You are mom, make a little happy moment for yourself and for your family.

_____
_____

Let us not become weary in doing good, for at the proper time we will reap a harvest if we do not give up. –Galatians 6:9

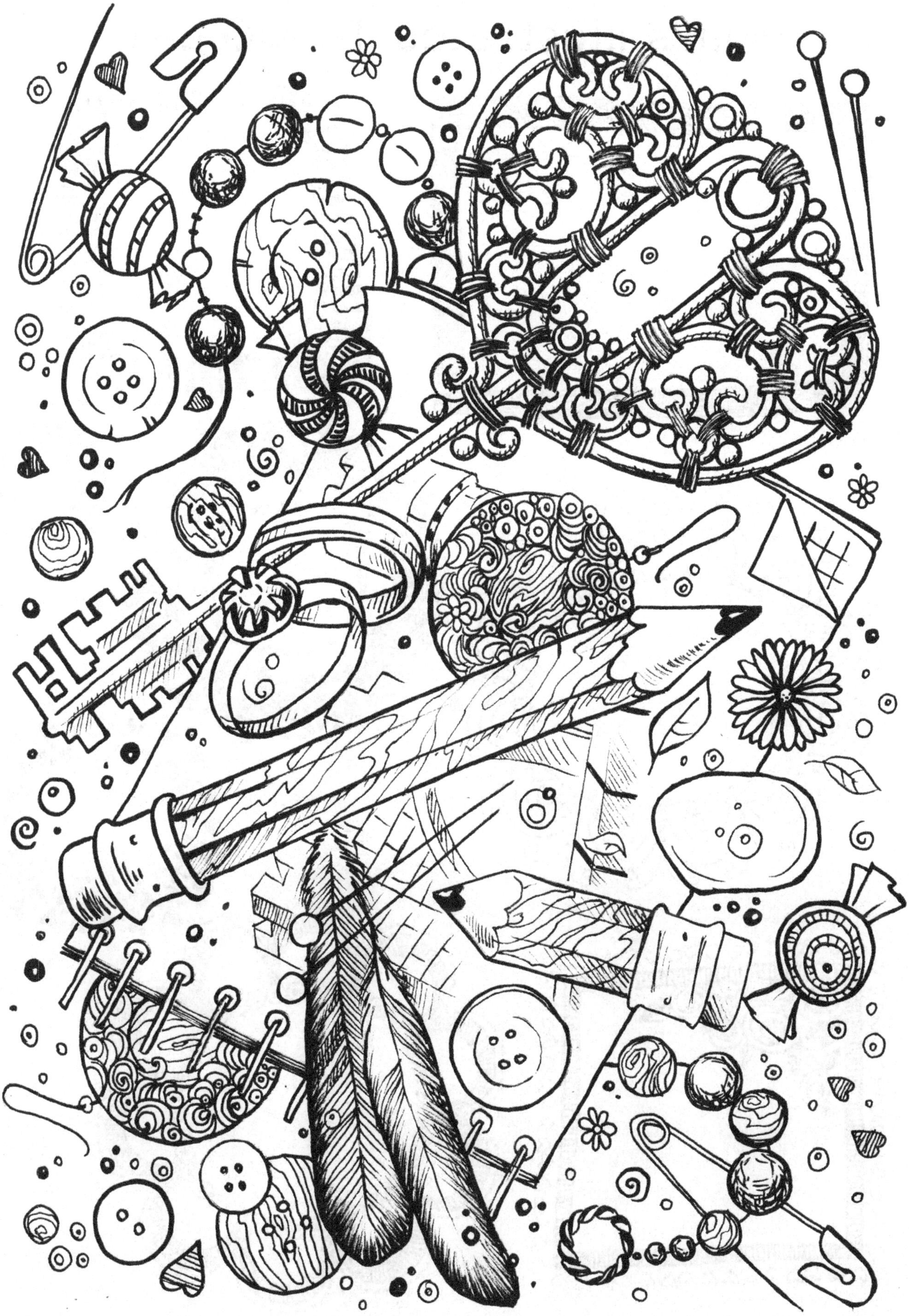

Mom's Illustrated TO-DO List

Menu Planning

Open up an old-fashion cookbook!

_____
_____
_____
_____
_____
_____

Shopping List

_____
_____
_____
_____
_____
_____
_____
_____
_____

Draw a Meal PLAN

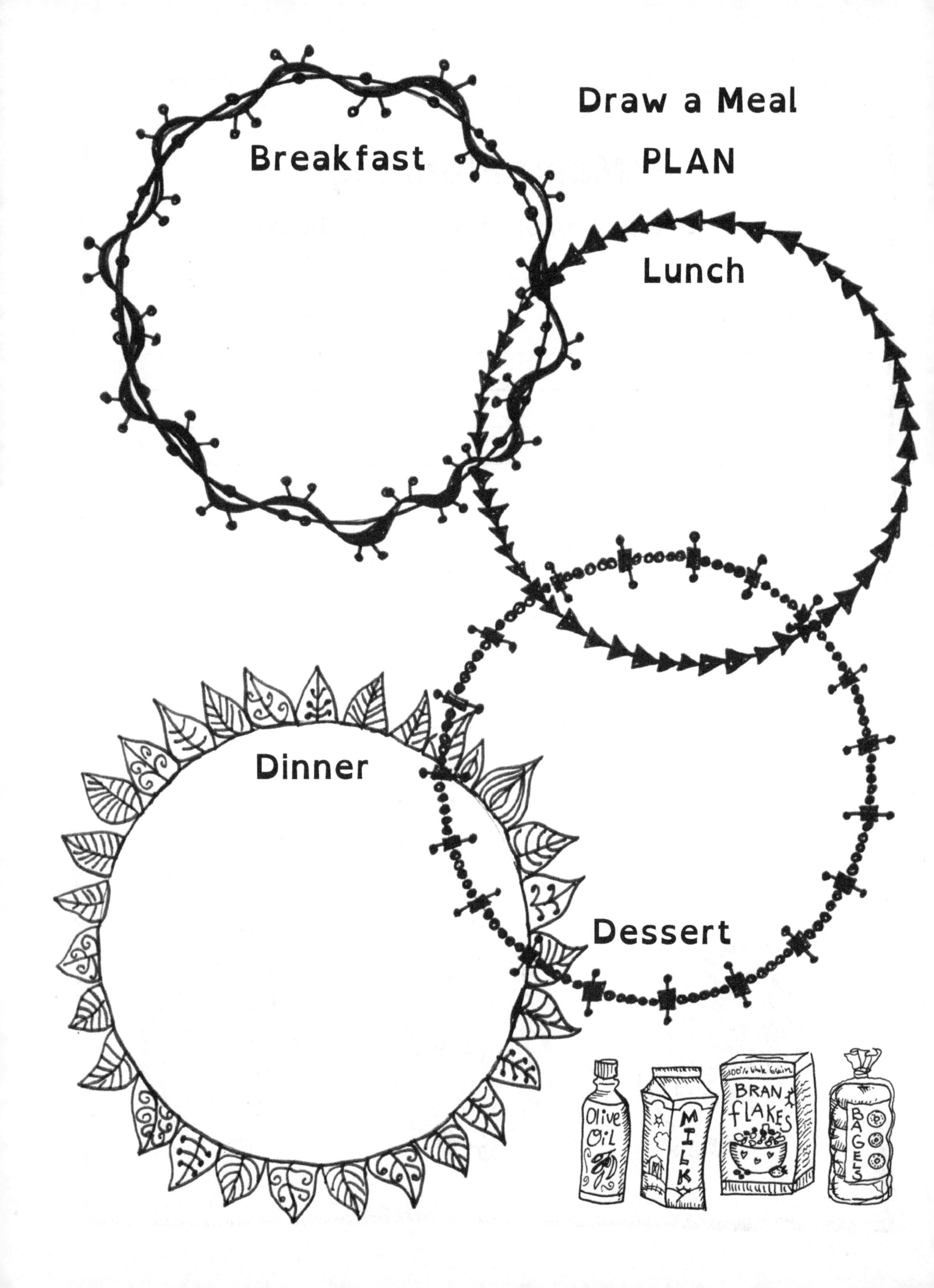

- Breakfast
- Lunch
- Dinner
- Dessert

Recipe:

3 Ingredient Pancakes

Serves: 6 people

Prep Time: 15 Minutes

Ingredients:

3 ripe bananas

6 eggs

1 tsp cinnamon

Instructions:

- In a bowl, combine the banana, eggs and cinnamon.
- Mix/mash until the mixture becomes all smooth. You can use a fork or a potato masher to achieve that.
- Grease your pan with a little bit of oil or butter.
- Heat your stove to a low to medium setting.
- Pour ¼ of the batter in your pan and cook for about 1½ minutes on both sides.
- Serve as is or garnish with anything you like banana slices with cinnamon and honey.

Shopping List:

"Recipe for genius: More of family and less of school, more of parents and less of peers, more creative freedom and less formal lessons." ~Raymond Moore

Mommy Math Time

Math is something that Kids need help with.

Go get a kid and show them how to do some math here:

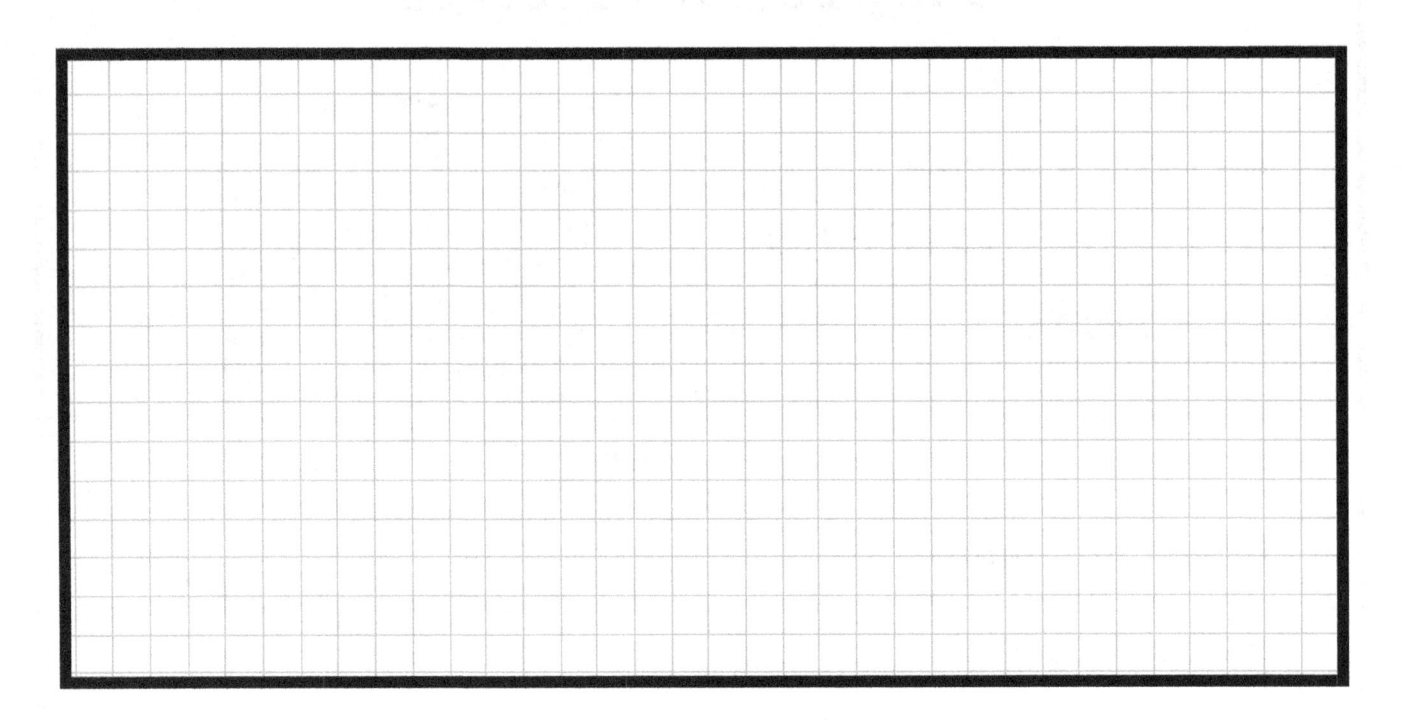

"Everything I am interested in, from cooking to electronics, is related to math. In real life you don't have to worry about integrating math into other subjects. In real life, math already is integrated into everything else." ~ Hoffstrom

Ideas for Fun & Learning Together

Reading Time

Sit down with a few books from your stack.

Write, draw or copy the things you want to remember.

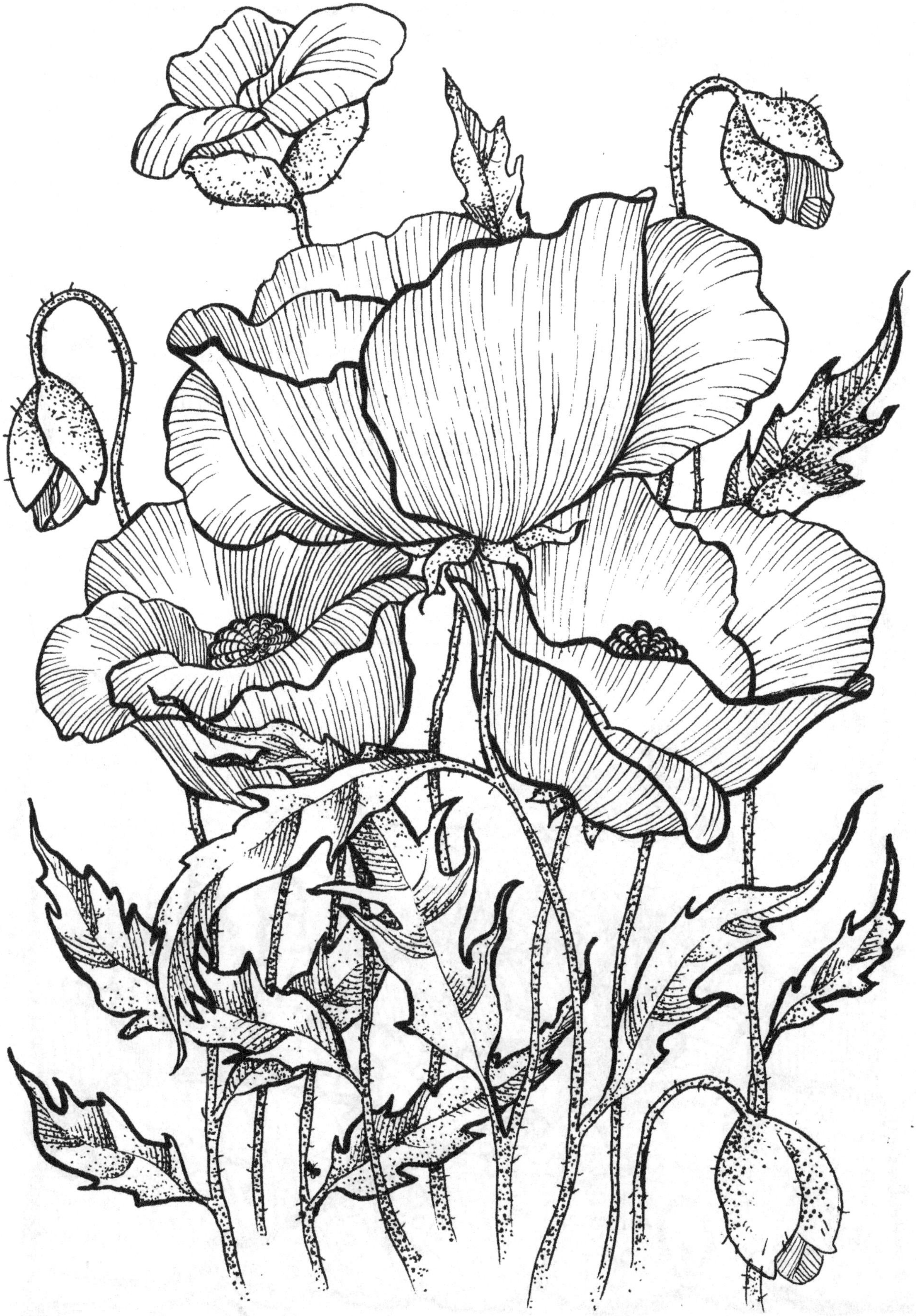

Listening Time

Listen to an audio book or classical music or ask someone to read a story to you while you color and draw on the next page.

What are you listening to?

_____

TITLE:

STARS:

Screen Time!
Watch a Documentary, Educational Program, Movie, or Tutorial.

My Review of this Film:

Draw a Scene from the video:

Rating:
AWFUL
BAD
LAME
YUCKY
OKAY
NICE
GOOD
GREAT
SUPER
AMAZING

World News Today!

Talk to your children about current events.
Look at a newspaper, news broadcast or website.
Color the countries teach them about.

Pray for the People and Communities
impacted by Bad News:

_____
_____
_____
_____
_____
_____
_____

Daily Journal

_____
_____
_____
_____
_____
_____
_____
_____
_____

"Education is not filling a bucket,
but lighting a fire." ~W.B. Yeats

Special Memories
Things that you want to remember...

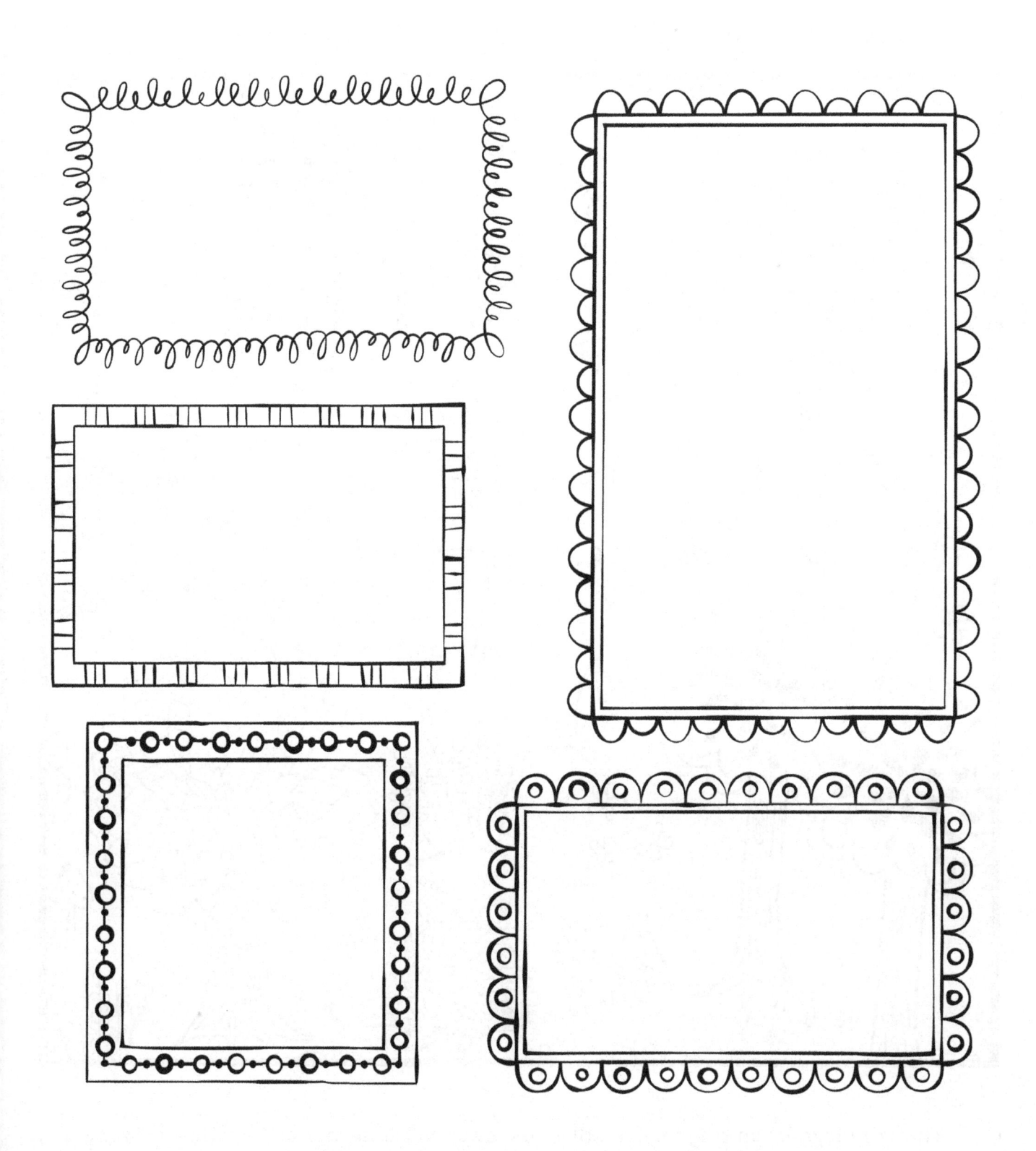

Mom's Coloring Time

Coloring beautiful pictures and doodling relieves stress and helps with creativity & relaxation.

"The true sign of intelligence is not knowledge but imagination." ~ Albert Einstein

A New Day!

My Verse, My Song or My Prayer...

What Matters Most...

Prayer List

Plans & Perspective

"The home is the first and most effective place to learn the lessons of life: truth, honor, virtue, self control, the value of education, honest work, and the purpose and privilege of life." - McKay

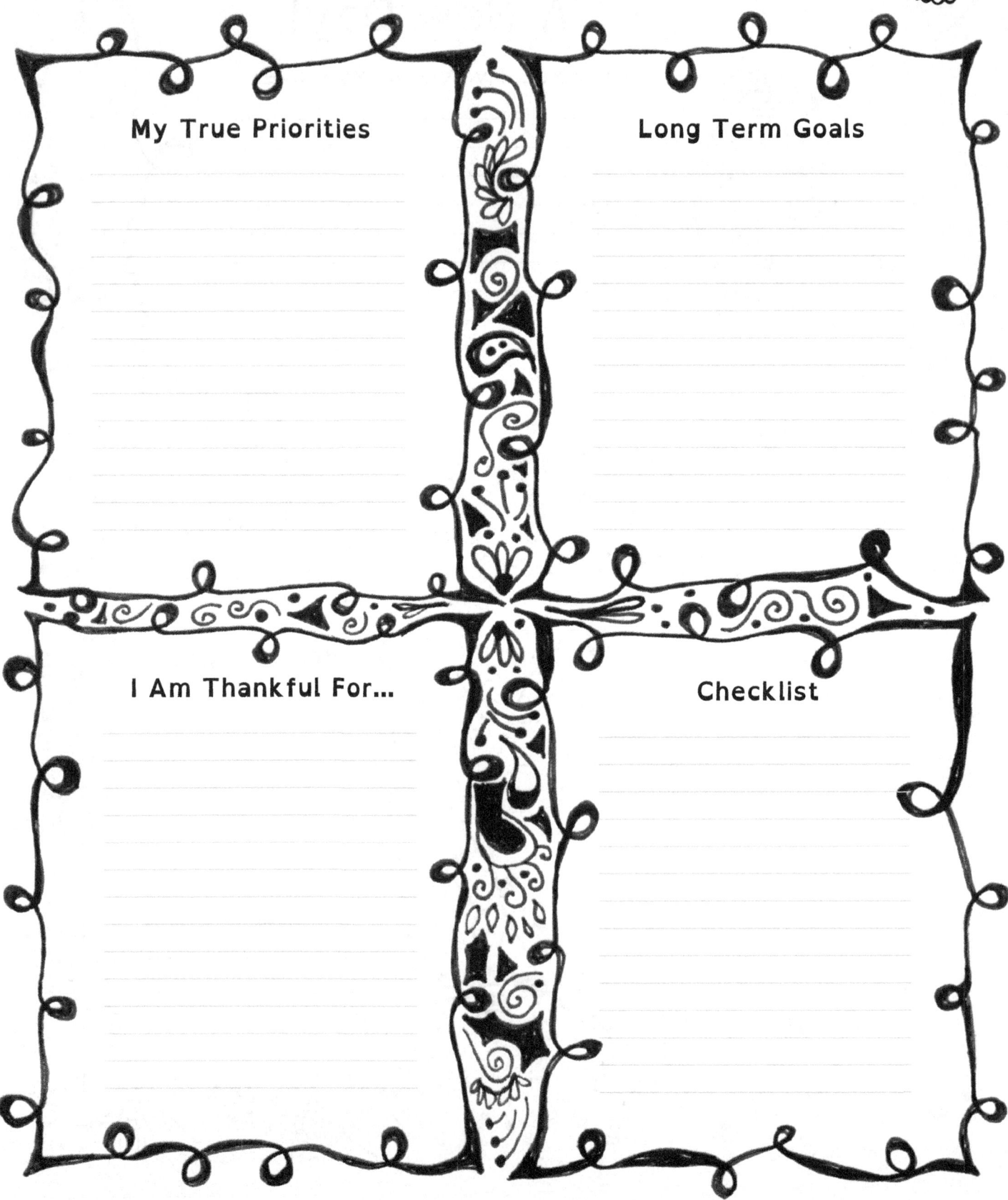

My True Priorities

Long Term Goals

I Am Thankful For...

Checklist

Attitude Improvement Time

How are your feeling today?
Color all the facial expressions that match your day!

| happy | surprised | joy | doubt | distrust |

| self-sufficiency | dreamy | shocked | scared | guile |

| gloomy | engrossment | flash | determination | thoughtful |

| diffidence | offence | confusion | craft | tired |

How is your mood influencing the people around you today?

_____

Do you need a cup of tea? Some chocolate? A hug? A quiet moment?
Peaceful music? Stop the clock. Make it happen. You are mom, make a little happy moment for yourself and for your family.

_____

Let us not become weary in doing good, for at the proper time we will reap a harvest if we do not give up. –Galatians 6:9

Reading Time

Sit down with a few books from your stack.

Write, draw or copy the things you want to remember.

Mom's Illustrated TO-DO List

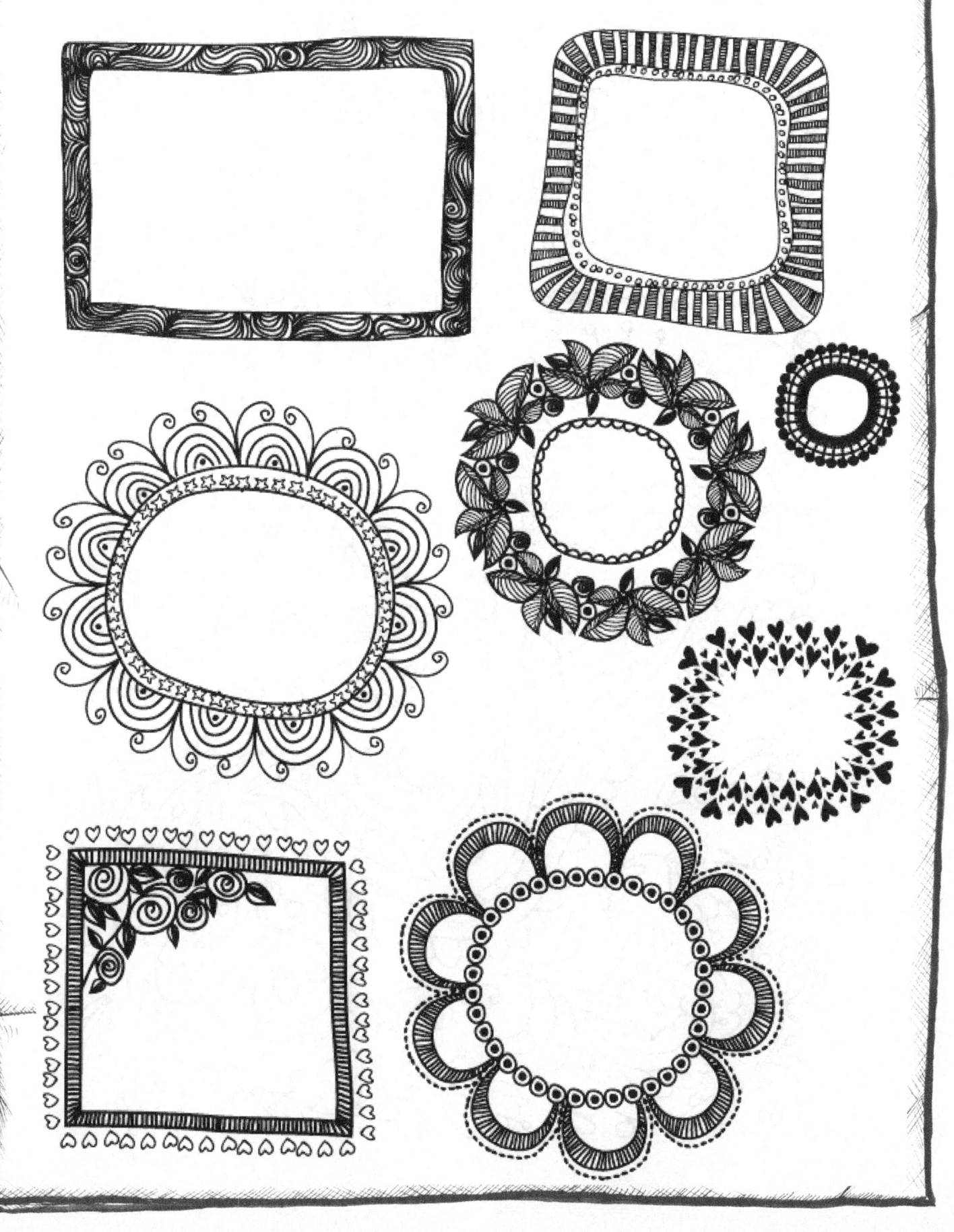

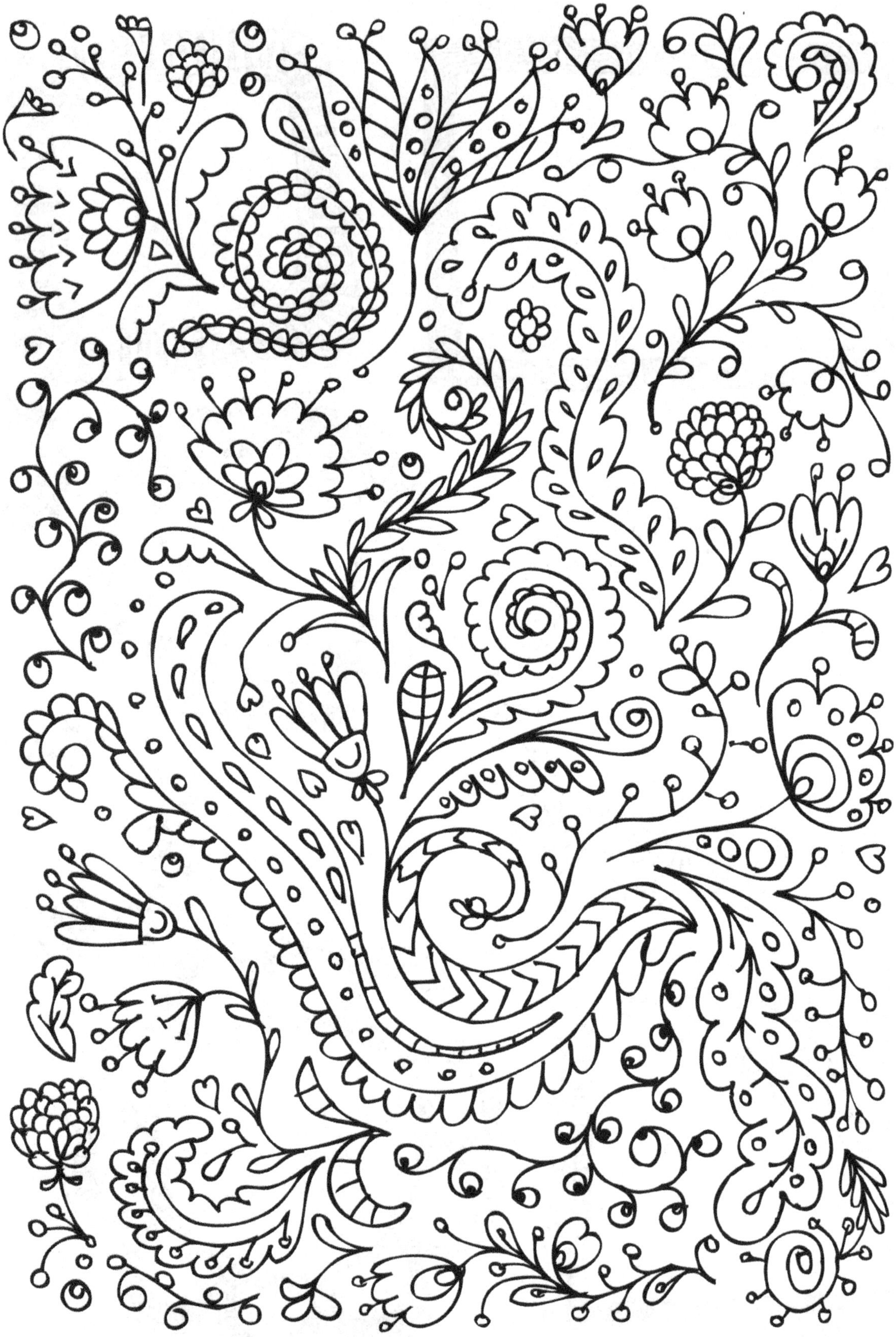

Ideas for Fun & Learning Together

Menu Planning
Open up an old-fashion cookbook!

_____
_____
_____
_____
_____
_____

Shopping List

_____
_____
_____
_____
_____
_____
_____
_____

Draw a Meal PLAN

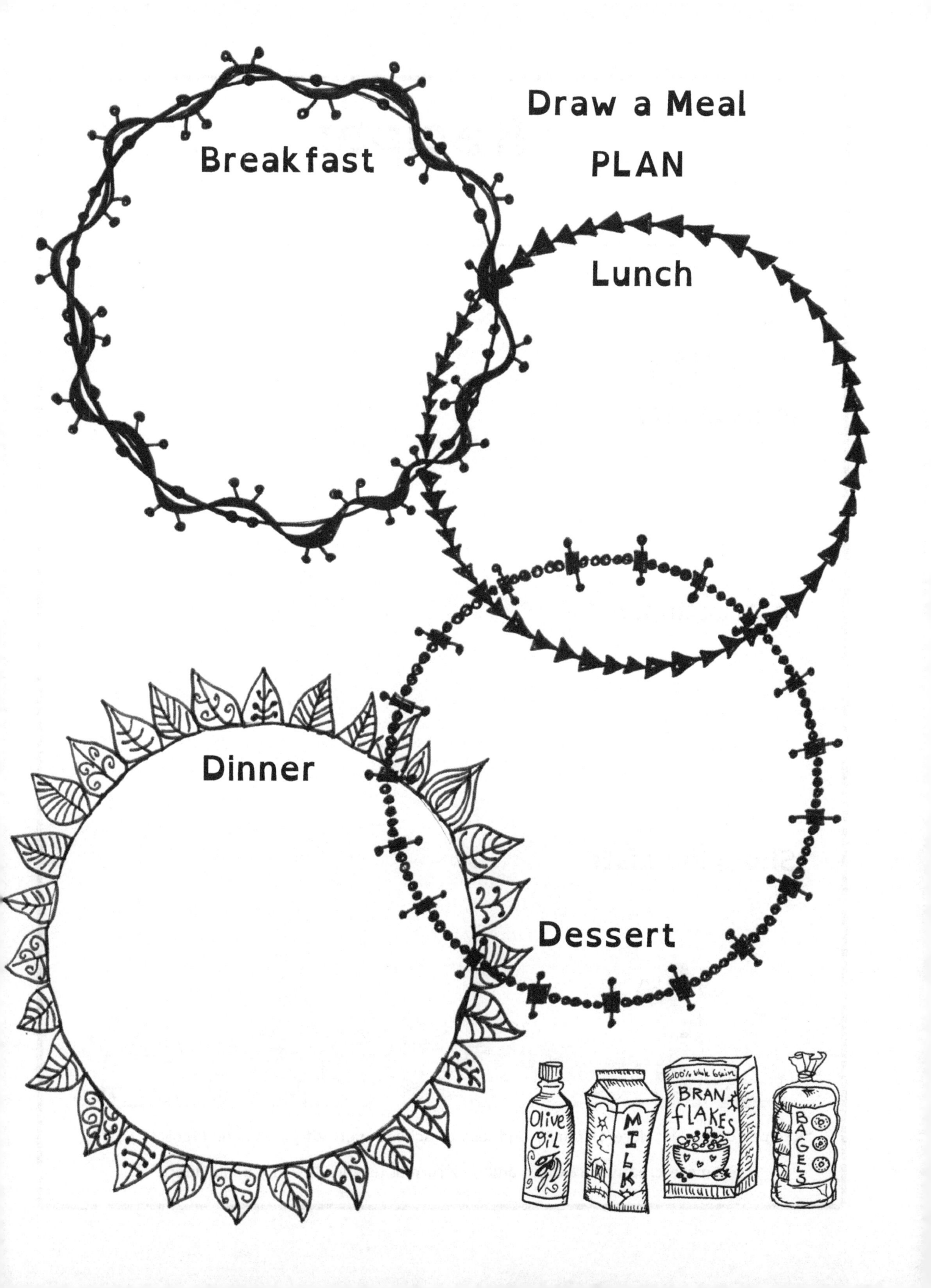

- Breakfast
- Lunch
- Dinner
- Dessert

Recipe:

_____

Serves:

Prep Time:

Ingredients:

Instructions:

Shopping List:

"Recipe for genius: More of family and less of school, more of parents and less of peers, more creative freedom and less formal lessons." ~Raymond Moore

A New Day!

My Verse, My Song or My Prayer...
_____
_____
_____
_____
_____
_____

What Matters Most...
_____
_____
_____
_____
_____

Prayer List
_____
_____
_____
_____
_____
_____
_____
_____

Mom's Coloring Time

Coloring beautiful pictures and doodling relieves stress and helps with creativity & relaxation.

"The true sign of intelligence is not knowledge but imagination." ~ Albert Einstein

Plans & Perspective

"The home is the first and most effective place to learn the lessons of life: truth, honor, virtue, self control, the value of education, honest work, and the purpose and privilege of life." - McKay

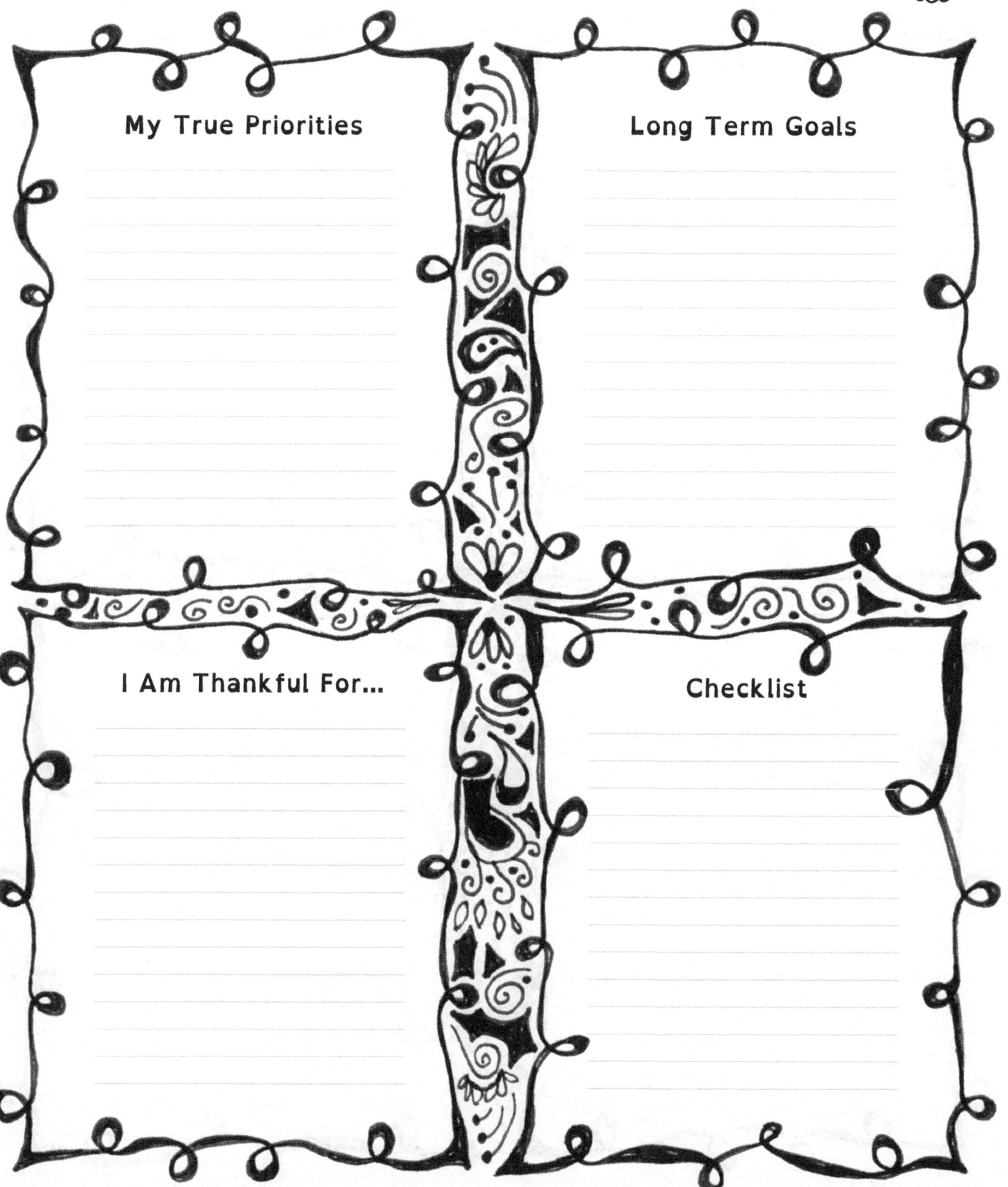

My True Priorities

Long Term Goals

I Am Thankful For...

Checklist

Reading Time

Sit down with a few books from your stack.
Write, draw or copy the things you want to remember.

Attitude Improvement Time

How are your feeling today?
Color all the facial expressions that match your day!

| happy | surprised | joy | doubt | distrust |

| self-sufficiency | dreamy | shocked | scared | guile |

| gloomy | engrossment | flash | determination | thoughtful |

| diffidence | offence | confusion | craft | tired |

How is your mood influencing the people around you today?
_____
_____

Do you need a cup of tea? Some chocolate? A hug? A quiet moment? Peaceful music? Stop the clock. Make it happen. You are mom. make a little happy moment for yourself and for your family.
_____
_____

Let us not become weary in doing good, for at the proper time we will reap a harvest if we do not give up. –Galatians 6:9

Reading Time

Sit down with a few books from your stack.

Write, draw or copy the things you want to remember.

Mom's Illustrated TO-DO List

Ideas for Fun & Learning Together

Menu Planning

Open up an old-fashion cookbook!

_____
_____
_____
_____
_____

Shopping List

_____
_____
_____
_____
_____
_____
_____

Draw a Meal PLAN

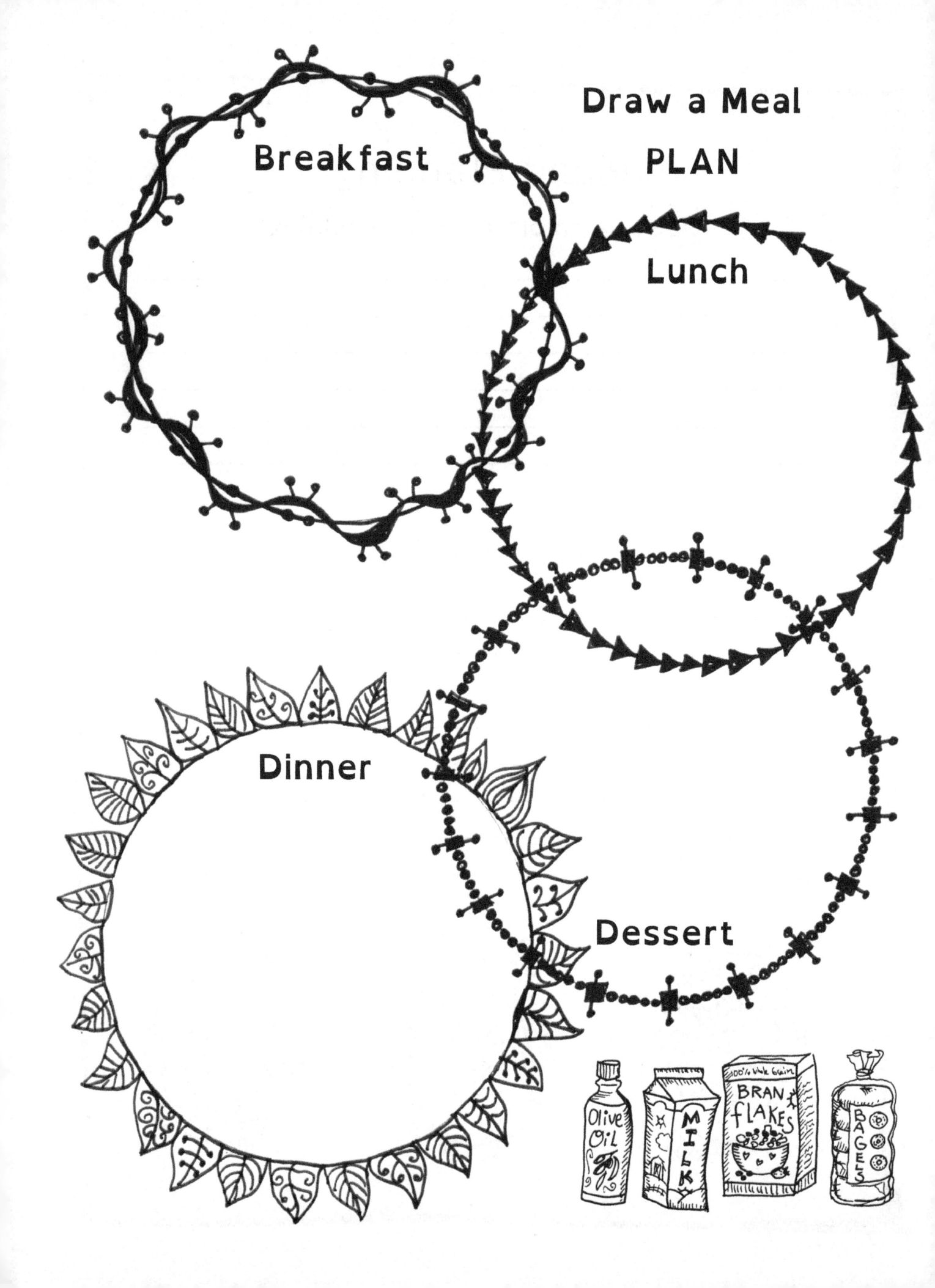

Breakfast

Lunch

Dinner

Dessert

Recipe:

_____

—

Serves:

Prep Time:

Ingredients:

Instructions:

Shopping List:

"Recipe for genius: More of family and less of school, more of parents and less of peers, more creative freedom and less formal lessons." ~Raymond Moore

Mommy Math Time

Math is something that Kids need help with.
Go get a kid and show them how to do some math here:

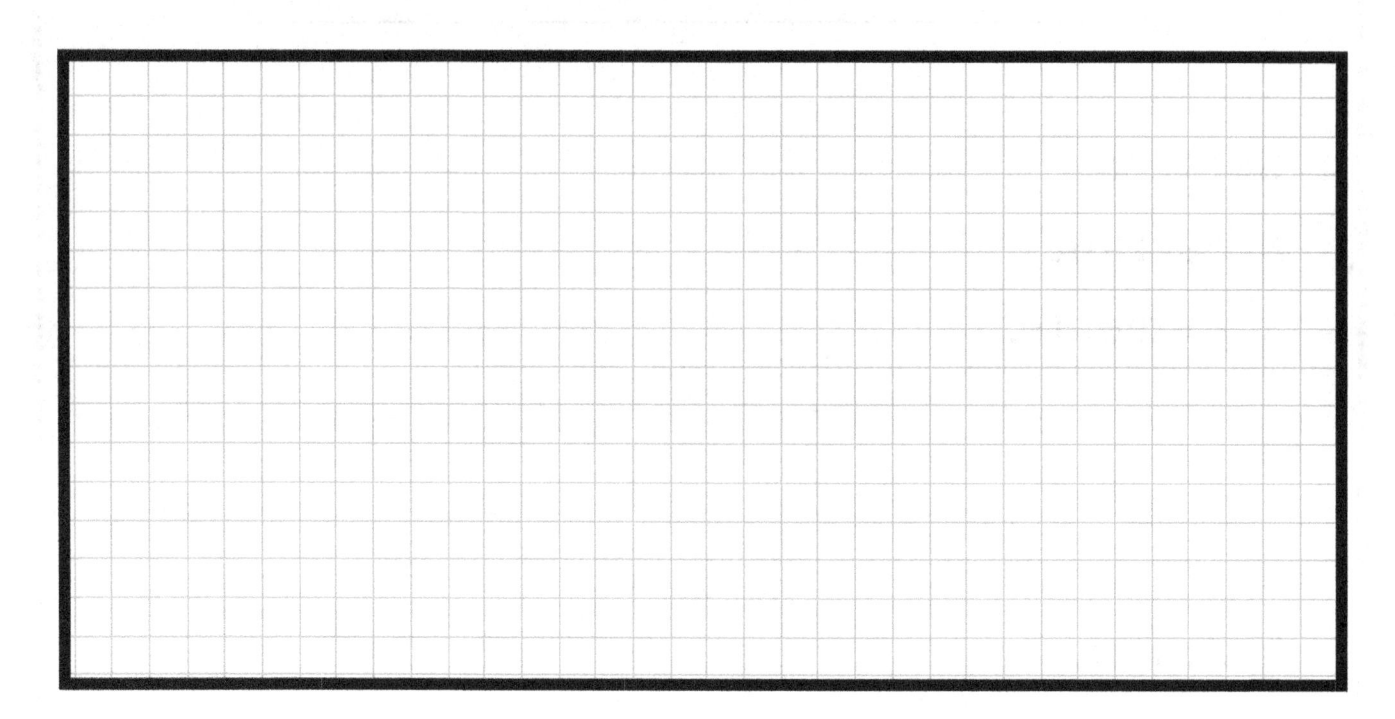

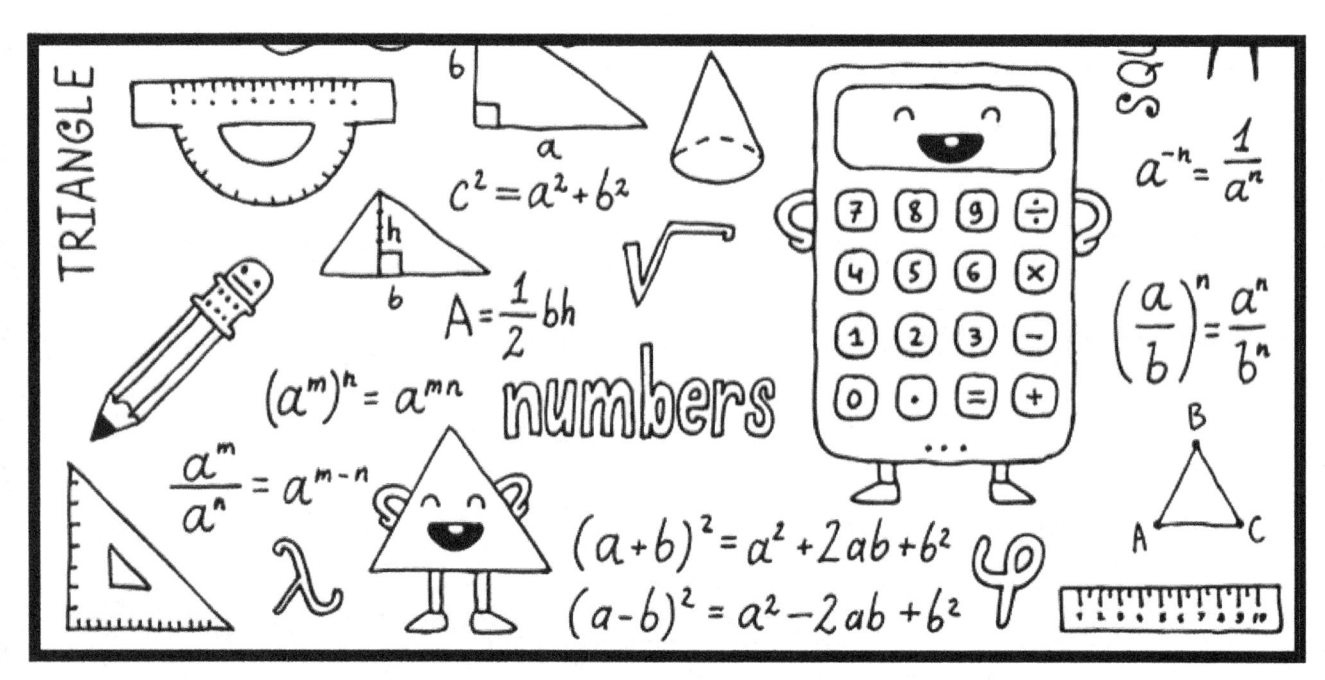

"Everything I am interested in, from cooking to electronics, is related to math. In real life you don't have to worry about integrating math into other subjects. In real life, math already is integrated into everything else." ~ Hoffstrom

Listening Time

Listen to an audio book or classical music or ask someone to read a story to you while you color and draw on the next page.

What are you listening to?

_____

Reading Time

Sit down with a few books from your stack.

Write, draw or copy the things you want to remember.

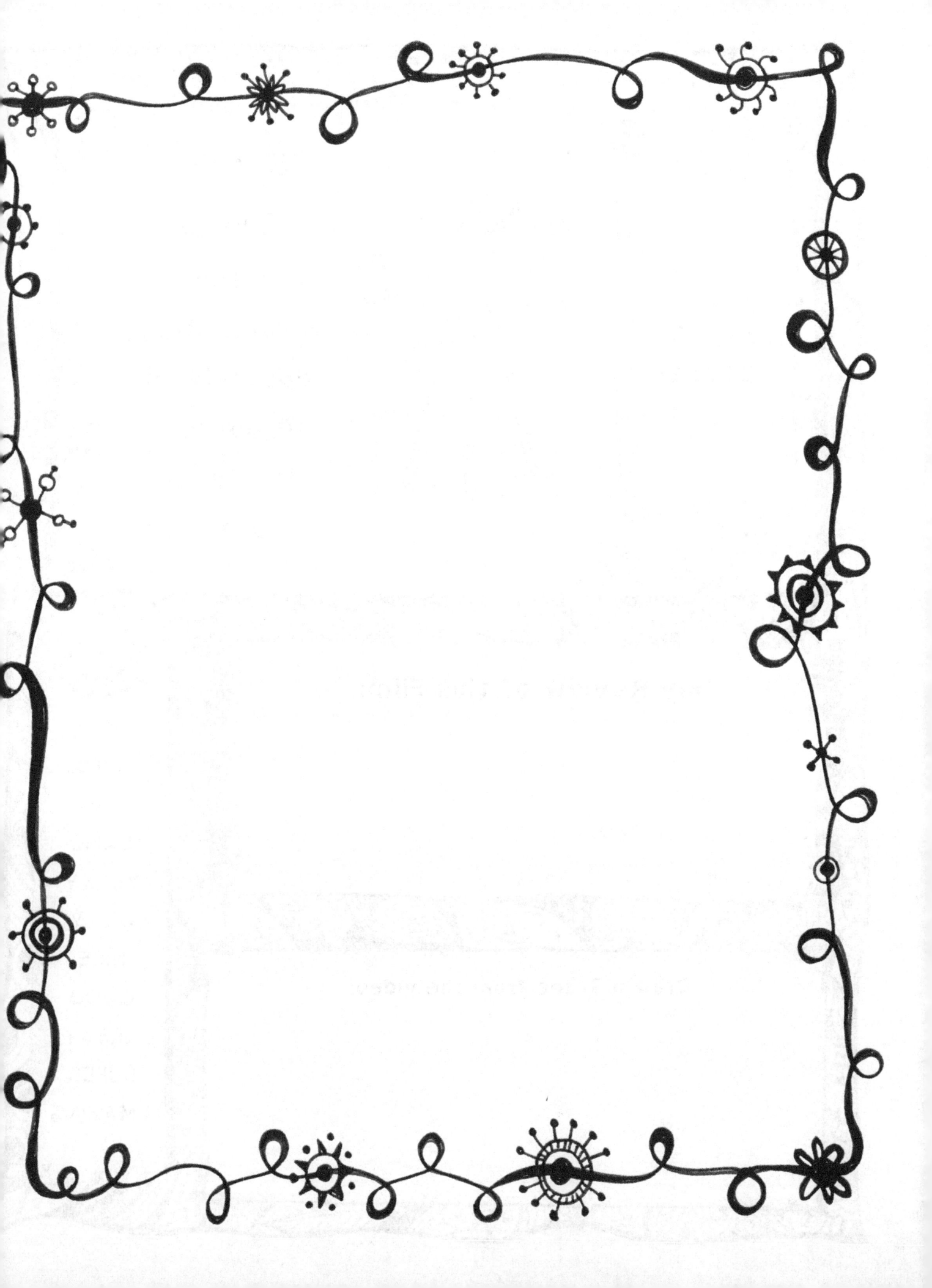

TITLE:

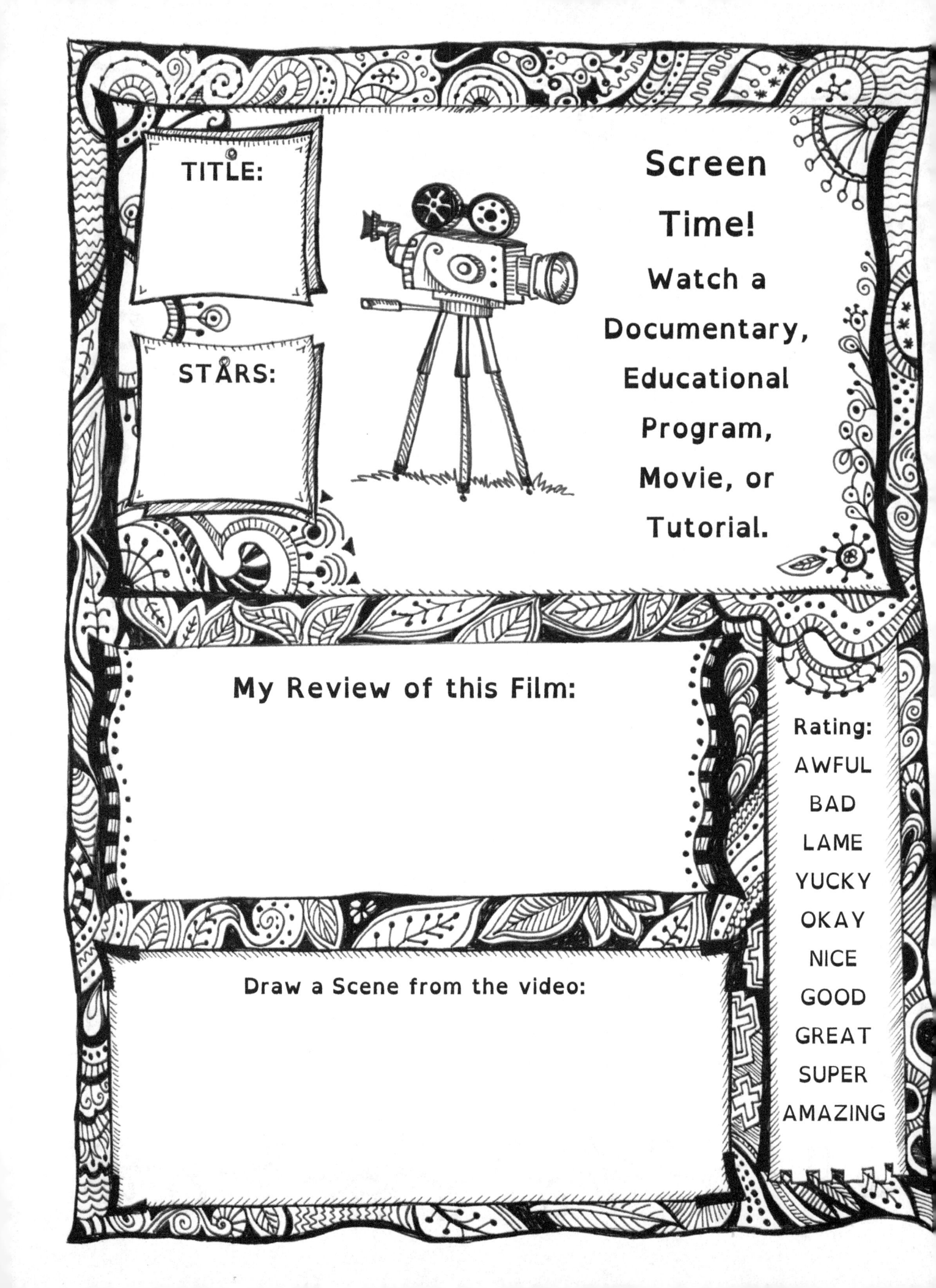

STARS:

Screen Time!

Watch a Documentary, Educational Program, Movie, or Tutorial.

My Review of this Film:

Rating:
AWFUL
BAD
LAME
YUCKY
OKAY
NICE
GOOD
GREAT
SUPER
AMAZING

Draw a Scene from the video:

World News Today!

Talk to your children about current events.
Look at a newspaper, news broadcast or website.
Color the countries teach them about.

Pray for the People and Communities
impacted by Bad News:

_____
_____
_____
_____
_____
_____
_____

Daily Journal

_____
_____
_____
_____
_____
_____
_____
_____
_____
_____
_____
_____

"Education is not filling a bucket,
but lighting a fire." ~W.B. Yeats

A New Day!

My Verse, My Song or My Prayer...

_____
_____
_____
_____
_____
_____

What Matters Most...

_____
_____
_____
_____

Prayer List

_____
_____
_____
_____
_____
_____
_____

Mom's Coloring Time

Coloring beautiful pictures and doodling relieves stress and helps with creativity & relaxation.

"The true sign of intelligence is not knowledge but imagination." ~ Albert Einstein

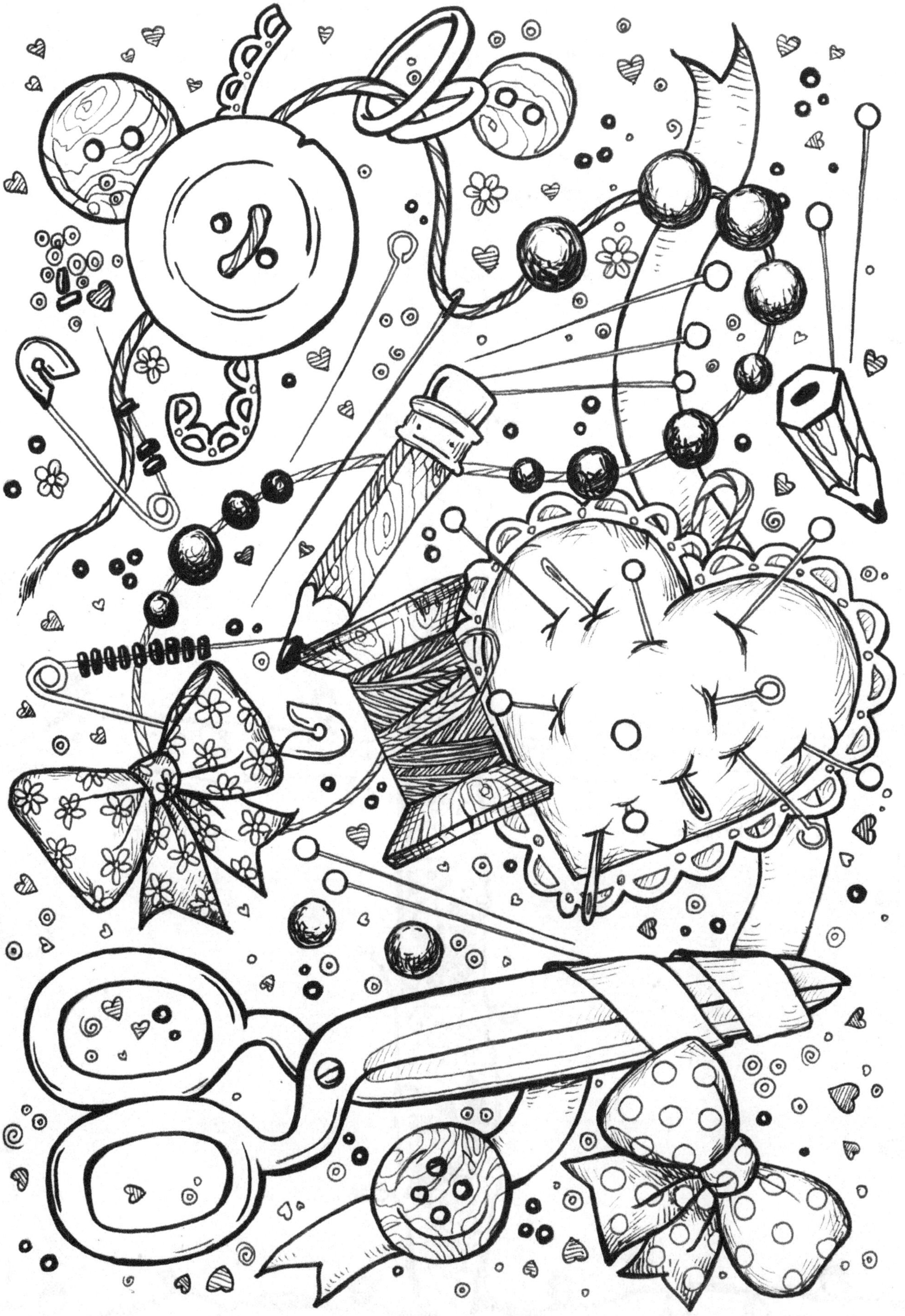

Plans & Perspective

"The home is the first and most effective place to learn the lessons of life: truth, honor, virtue, self control, the value of education, honest work, and the purpose and privilege of life." - McKay

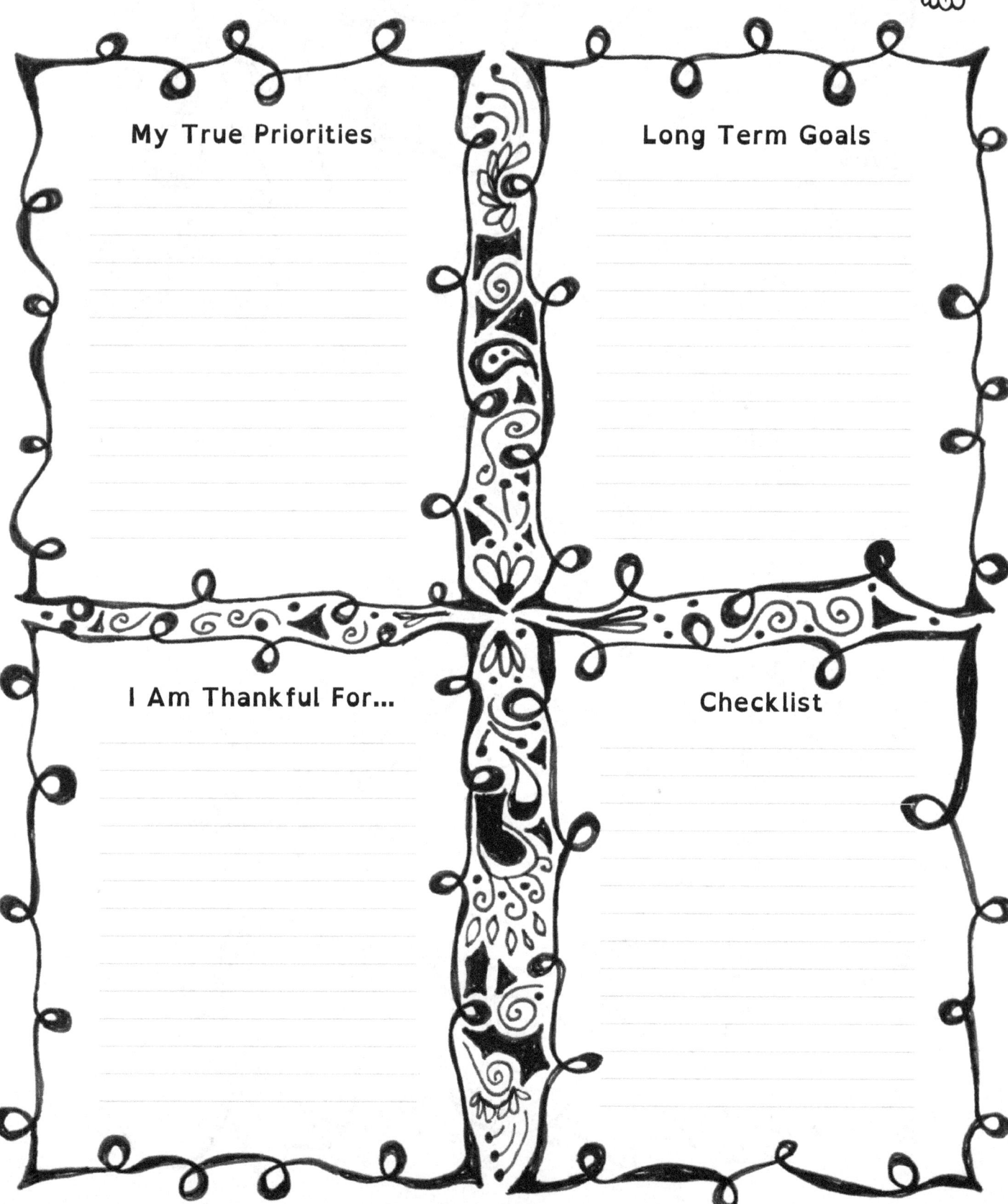

My True Priorities

Long Term Goals

I Am Thankful For...

Checklist

Attitude Improvement Time

How are your feeling today?
Color all the facial expressions that match your day!

| happy | surprised | joy | doubt | distrust |

| self-sufficiency | dreamy | shocked | scared | guile |

| gloomy | engrossment | flash | determination | thoughtful |

| diffidence | offence | confusion | craft | tired |

How is your mood influencing the people around you today?

_____

Do you need a cup of tea? Some chocolate? A hug? A quiet moment? Peaceful music? Stop the clock. Make it happen. You are mom. make a little happy moment for yourself and for your family.

_____

Let us not become weary in doing good, for at the proper time we will reap a harvest if we do not give up. —Galatians 6:9

Reading Time

Sit down with a few books from your stack.

Write, draw or copy the things you want to remember.

Reading Time

Sit down with a few books from your stack.

Write, draw or copy the things you want to remember.

Mom's Illustrated TO-DO List

Ideas for Fun & Learning Together

Menu Planning

Open up an old-fashion cookbook!

_____
_____
_____
_____
_____

Shopping List

_____
_____
_____
_____
_____
_____
_____
_____
_____

A New Day!

My Verse, My Song or My Prayer...
_____
_____
_____
_____
_____
_____

What Matters Most...
_____
_____
_____
_____
_____

Prayer List
_____
_____
_____
_____
_____
_____
_____

Mom's Coloring Time

Coloring beautiful pictures and doodling relieves stress and helps with creativity & relaxation.

"The true sign of intelligence is not knowledge but imagination." ~ Albert Einstein

Plans & Perspective

"The home is the first and most effective place to learn the lessons of life: truth, honor, virtue, self control, the value of education, honest work, and the purpose and privilege of life." - McKay

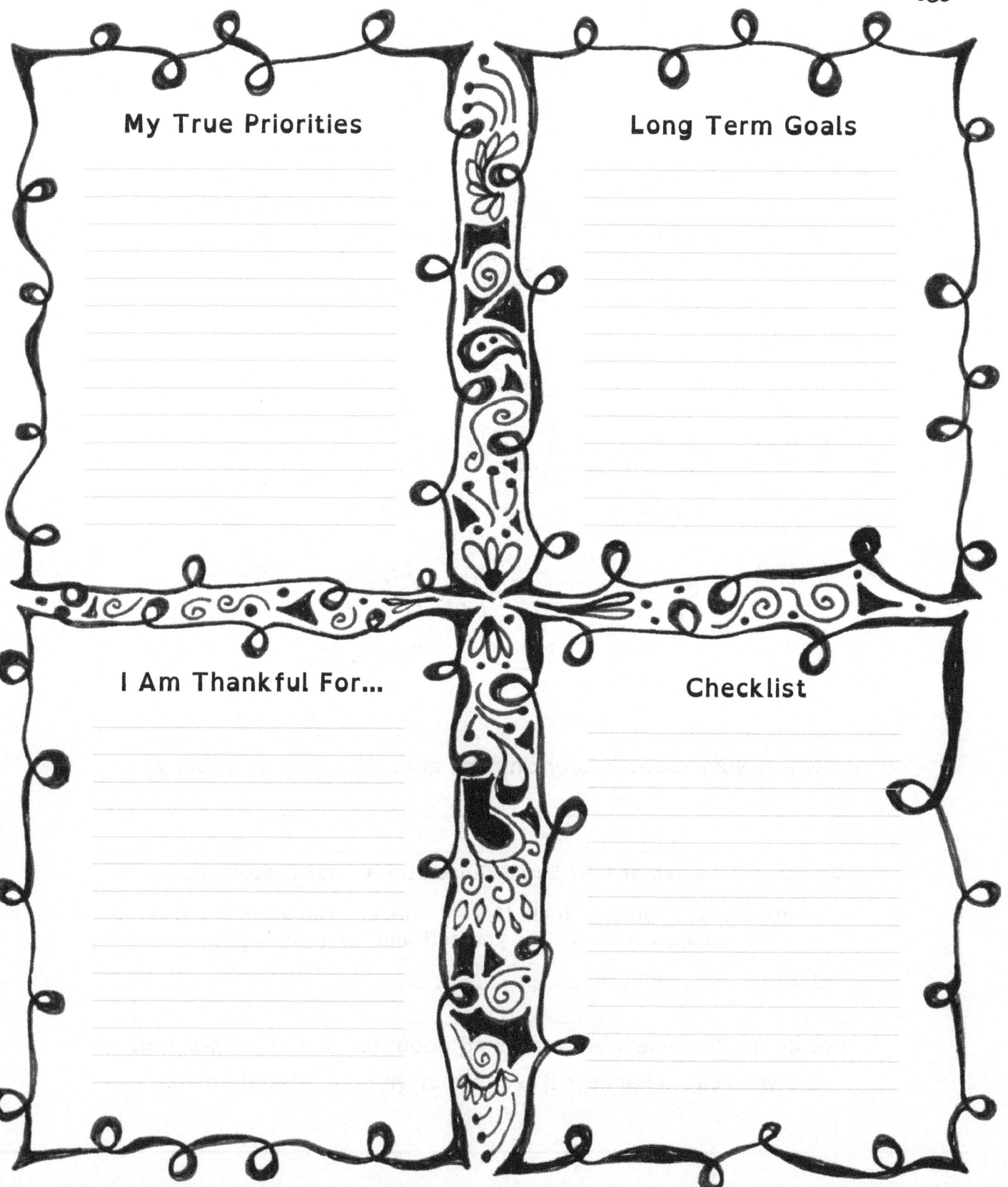

My True Priorities

Long Term Goals

I Am Thankful For...

Checklist

Attitude Improvement Time

How are your feeling today?

Color all the facial expressions that match your day!

happy	surprised	joy	doubt	distrust
self-sufficiency	dreamy	shocked	scared	guile
gloomy	engrossment	flash	determination	thoughtful
diffidence	offence	confusion	craft	tired

How is your mood influencing the people around you today?

___

Do you need a cup of tea? Some chocolate? A hug? A quiet moment?

Peaceful music? Stop the clock. Make it happen. You are mom, make a little happy moment for yourself and for your family.

___

Let us not become weary in doing good, for at the proper time we will reap a harvest if we do not give up. –Galatians 6:9

Reading Time

Sit down with a few books from your stack.

Write, draw or copy the things you want to remember.

Mom's Illustrated TO-DO List

Reading Time

Sit down with a few books from your stack.

Write, draw or copy the things you want to remember.

Ideas for Fun & Learning Together

Menu Planning

Open up an old-fashion cookbook!

_____
_____
_____
_____
_____

Shopping List

_____
_____
_____
_____
_____
_____
_____

Draw a Meal PLAN

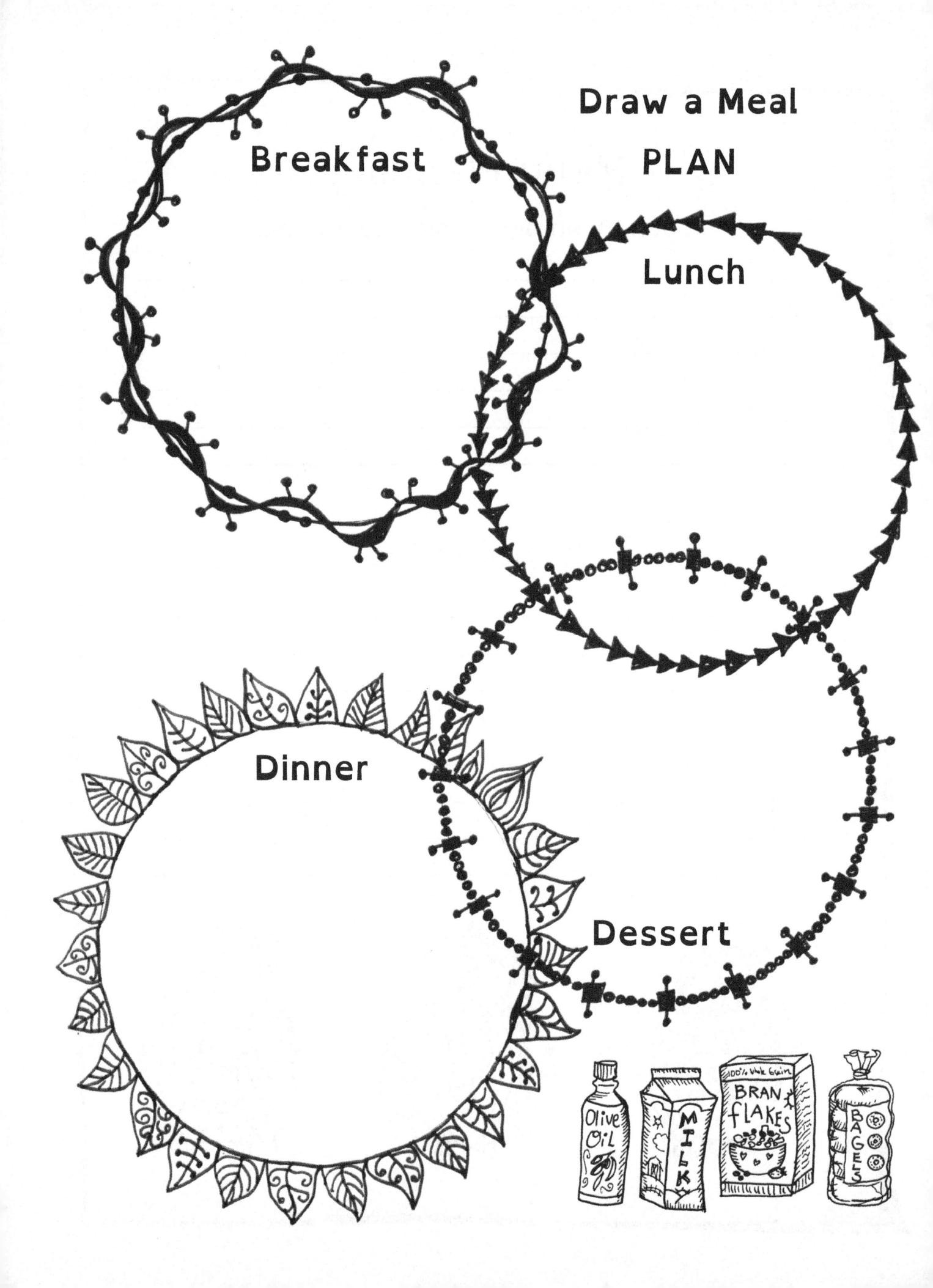

- Breakfast
- Lunch
- Dinner
- Dessert

Recipe:

_____

Serves:

Prep Time:

Ingredients:

Instructions:

Shopping List:

"Recipe for genius: More of family and less of school, more of parents and less of peers, more creative freedom and less formal lessons." ~Raymond Moore

Mommy Math Time

Math is something that Kids need help with.
Go get a kid and show them how to do some math here:

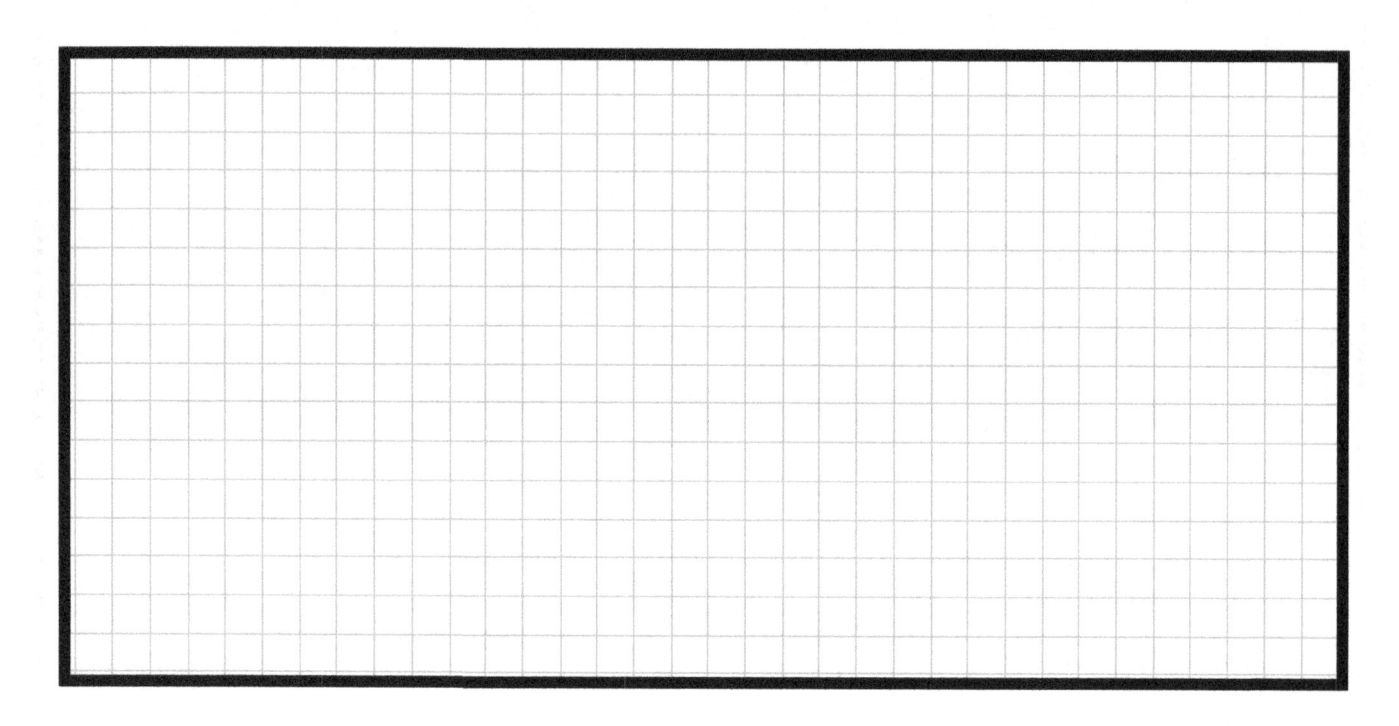

"Everything I am interested in, from cooking to electronics, is related to math. In real life you don't have to worry about integrating math into other subjects. In real life, math already is integrated into everything else." ~ Hoffstrom

Listening Time

Listen to an audio book or classical music or ask someone to read a story to you while you color and draw on the next page.

What are you listening to?

_____

TITLE:

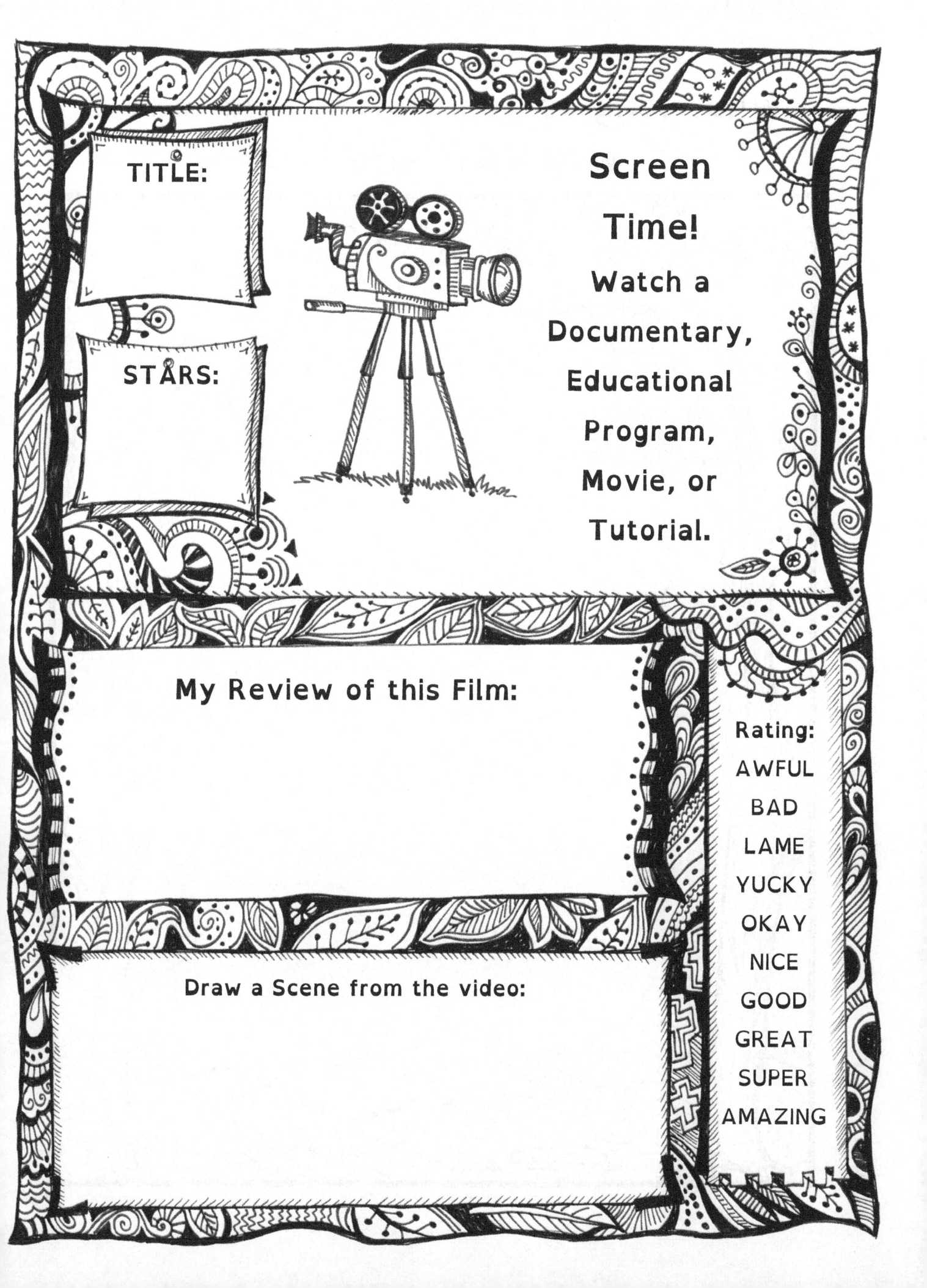

STARS:

Screen Time!

Watch a Documentary, Educational Program, Movie, or Tutorial.

My Review of this Film:

Rating:
AWFUL
BAD
LAME
YUCKY
OKAY
NICE
GOOD
GREAT
SUPER
AMAZING

Draw a Scene from the video:

What song do you want to sing today?
Write a few verses here:

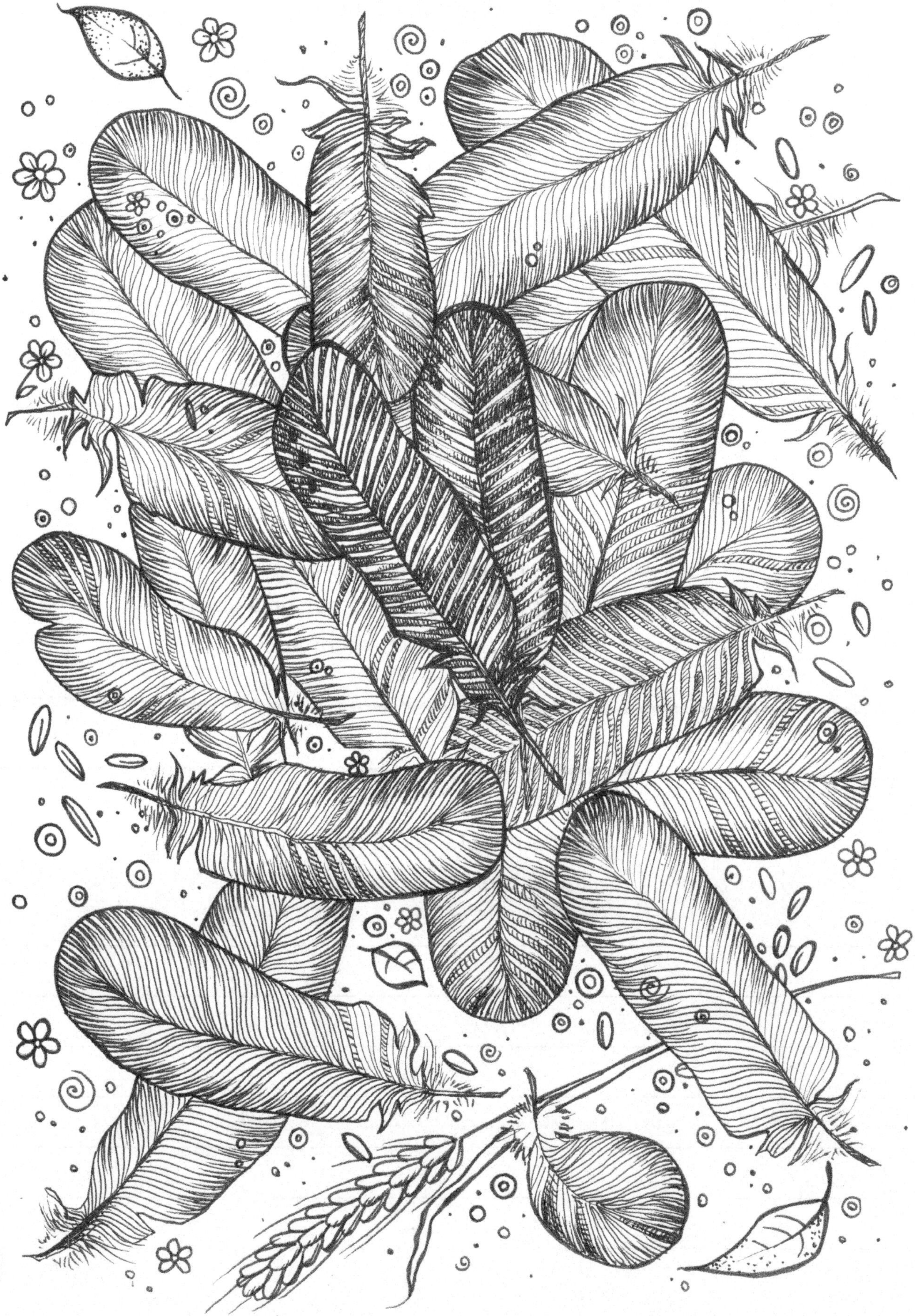

World News Today!

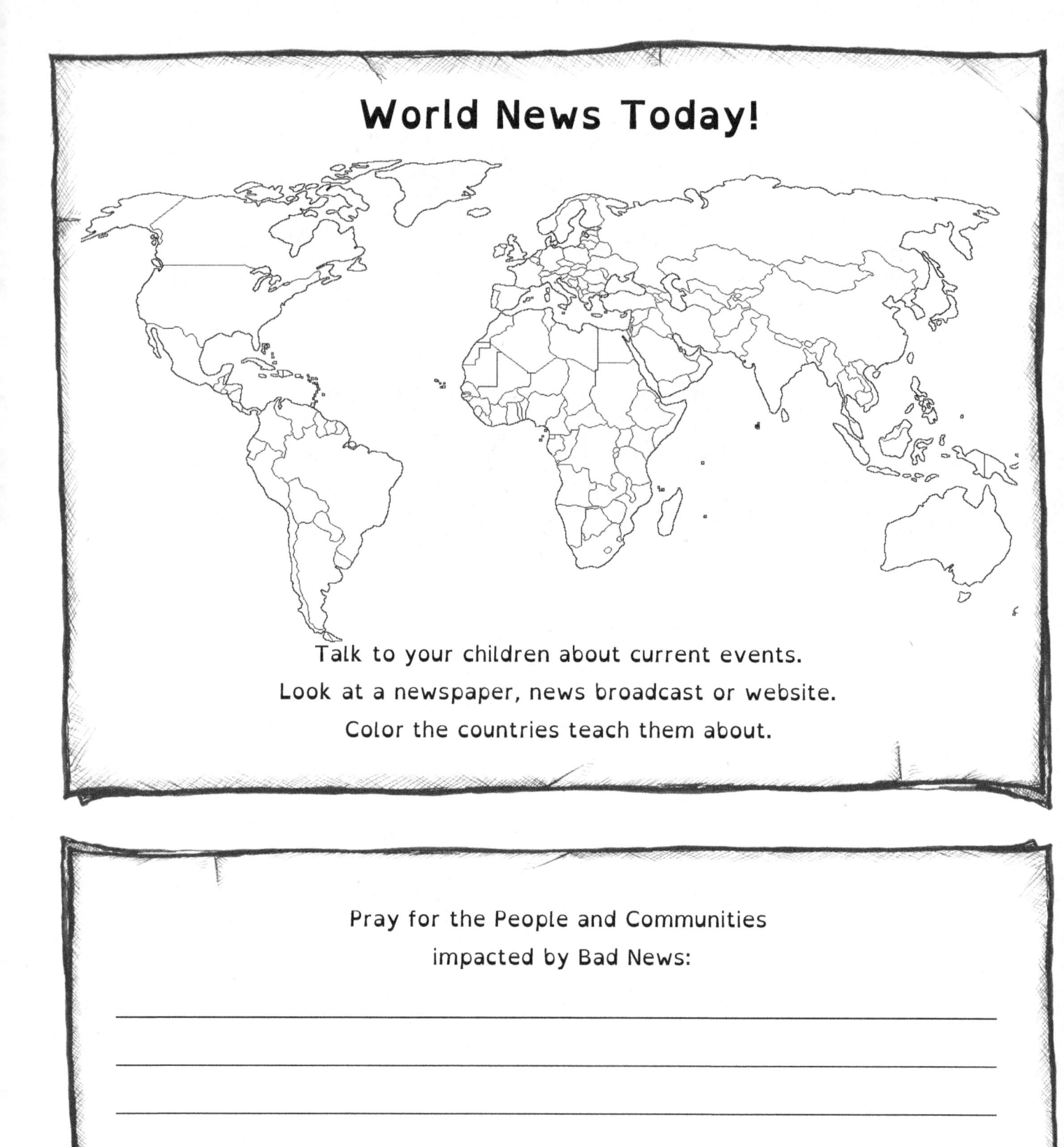

Talk to your children about current events.
Look at a newspaper, news broadcast or website.
Color the countries teach them about.

Pray for the People and Communities
impacted by Bad News:

_____
_____
_____
_____
_____
_____
_____

Reading Time

Sit down with a few books from your stack.

Write, draw or copy the things you want to remember.

Daily Journal

_____
_____
_____
_____
_____
_____
_____
_____
_____
_____
_____

"Education is not filling a bucket,
but lighting a fire." ~W.B. Yeats

A New Day!

My Verse, My Song or My Prayer...
_____
_____
_____
_____
_____
_____
_____

What Matters Most...
_____
_____
_____
_____
_____

Prayer List
_____
_____
_____
_____
_____
_____
_____
_____

Mom's Coloring Time

Coloring beautiful pictures and doodling relieves stress and helps with creativity & relaxation.

"The true sign of intelligence is not knowledge but imagination." ~ Albert Einstein

Plans & Perspective

"The home is the first and most effective place to learn the lessons of life: truth, honor, virtue, self control, the value of education, honest work, and the purpose and privilege of life." - McKay

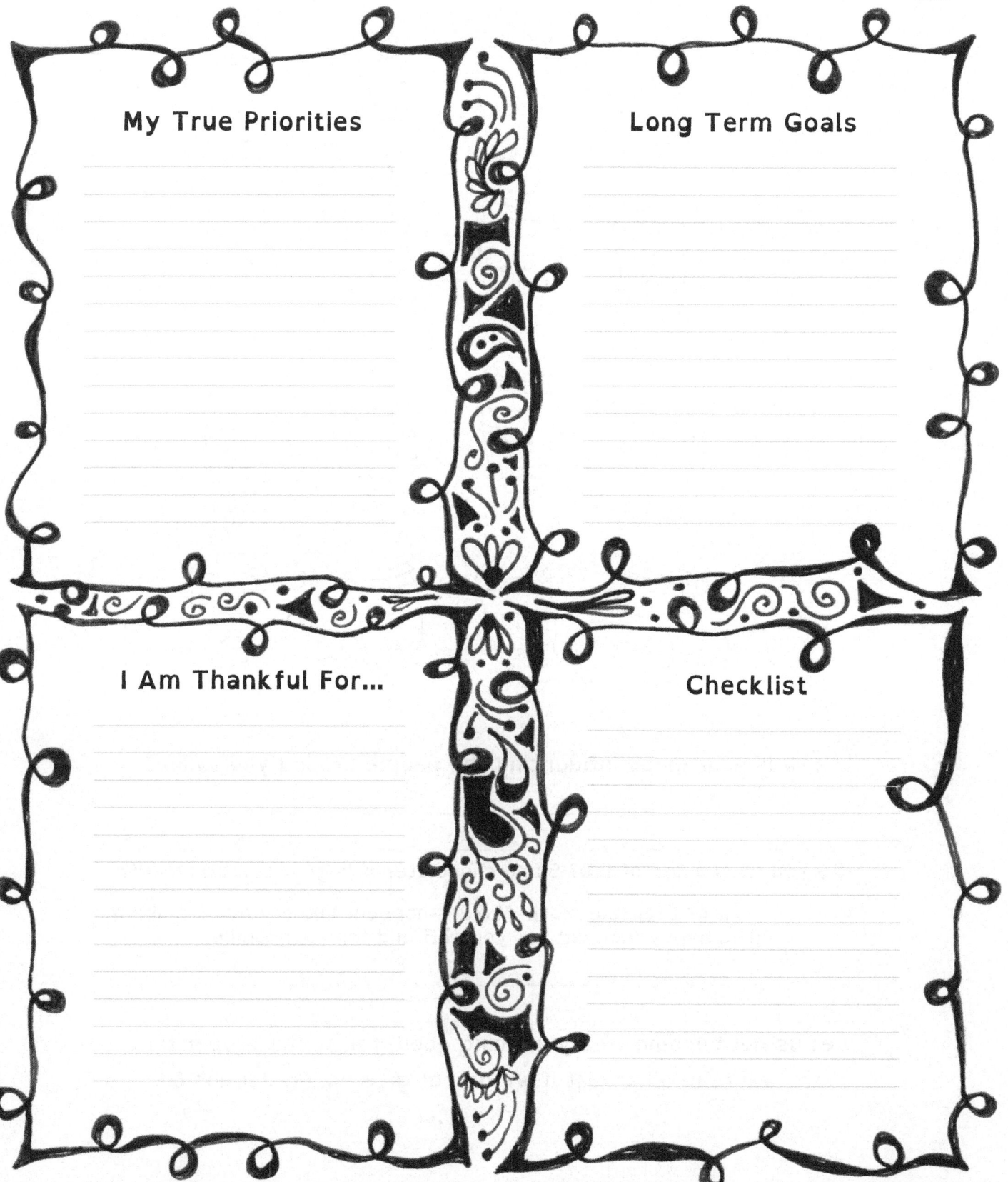

My True Priorities

Long Term Goals

I Am Thankful For...

Checklist

Attitude Improvement Time

How are your feeling today?
Color all the facial expressions that match your day!

happy	surprised	joy	doubt	distrust

self-sufficiency	dreamy	shocked	scared	guile

gloomy	engrossment	flash	determination	thoughtful

diffidence	offence	confusion	craft	tired

How is your mood influencing the people around you today?
_____
_____

Do you need a cup of tea? Some chocolate? A hug? A quiet moment?

Peaceful music? Stop the clock. Make it happen. You are mom, make a little happy moment for yourself and for your family.
_____
_____

Let us not become weary in doing good, for at the proper time we will reap a harvest if we do not give up. —Galatians 6:9

Reading Time

Sit down with a few books from your stack.

Write, draw or copy the things you want to remember.

Mom's Illustrated TO-DO List

Ideas for Fun & Learning Together

Menu Planning

Open up an old-fashion cookbook!

_____
_____
_____
_____
_____
_____

Shopping List

_____
_____
_____
_____
_____
_____
_____
_____

Reading Time

Sit down with a few books from your stack.

Write, draw or copy the things you want to remember.

Draw a Meal PLAN

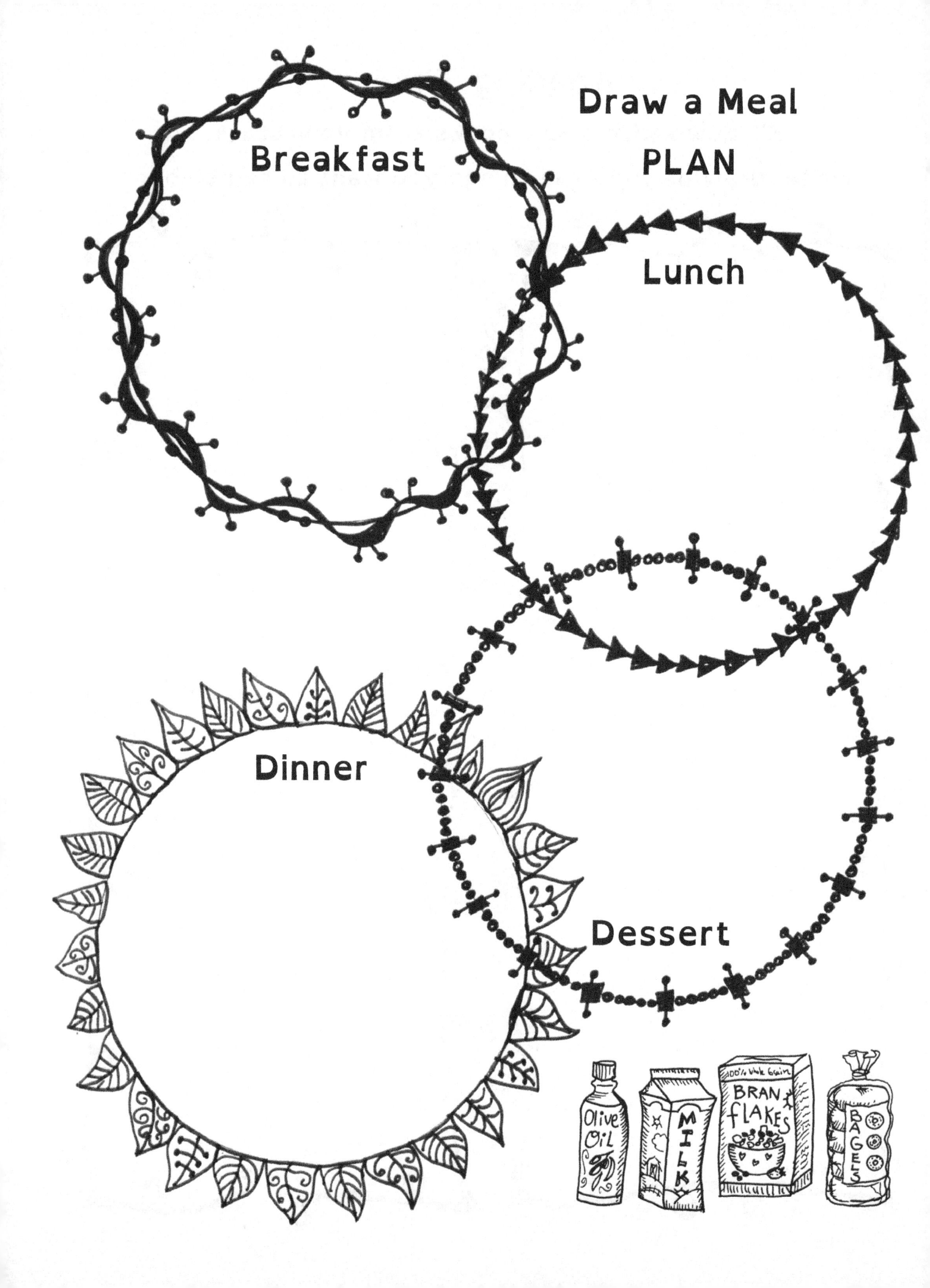

- Breakfast
- Lunch
- Dinner
- Dessert

Recipe:

_____

Serves:

Prep Time:

Ingredients:

Instructions:

Shopping List:

"Recipe for genius: More of family and less of school, more of parents and less of peers, more creative freedom and less formal lessons." ~Raymond Moore

Mommy Math Time

Math is something that Kids need help with.

Go get a kid and show them how to do some math here:

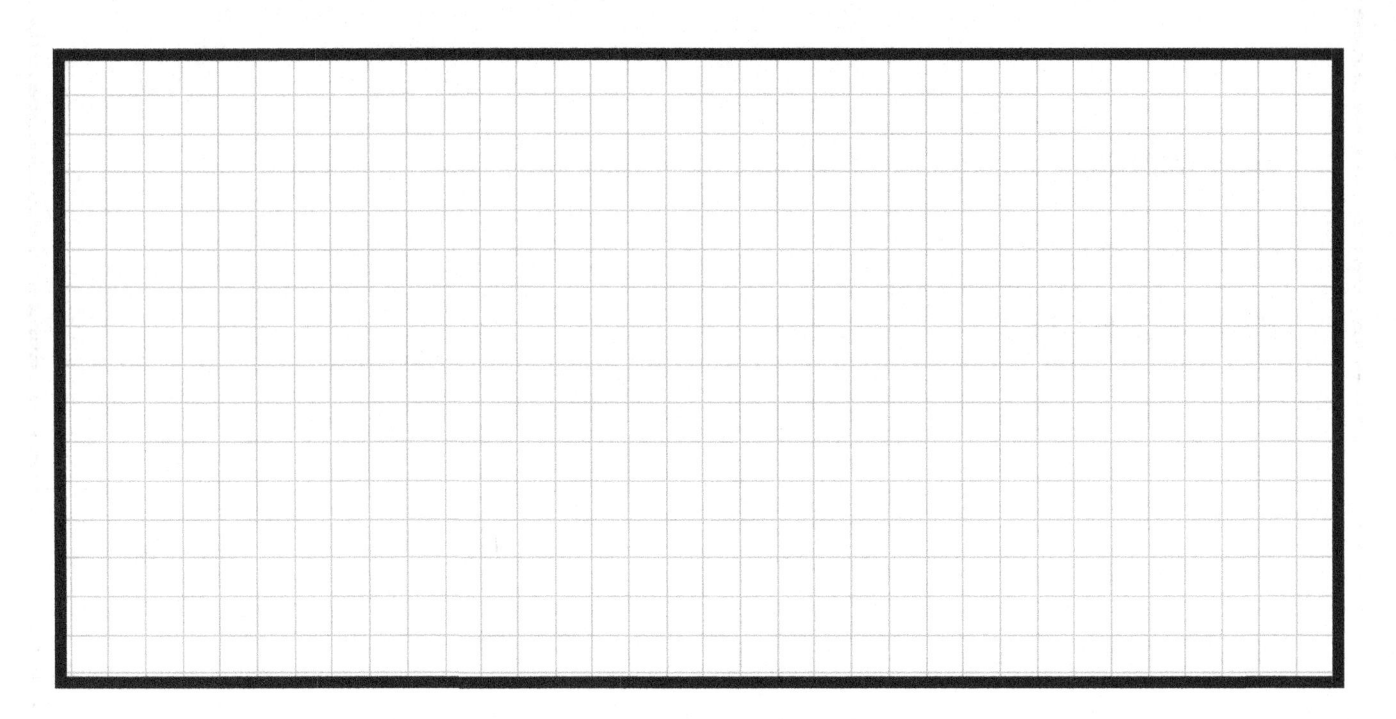

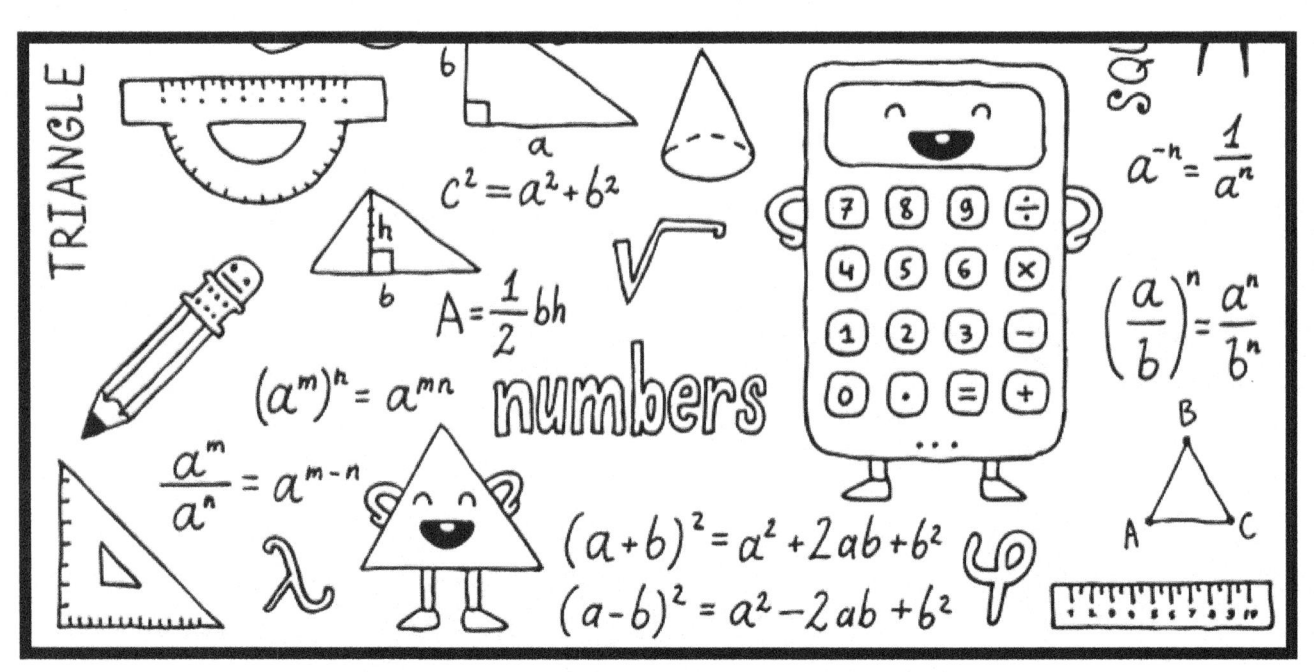

"Everything I am interested in, from cooking to electronics, is related to math. In real life you don't have to worry about integrating math into other subjects. In real life, math already is integrated into everything else." ~ Hoffstrom

Listening Time

Listen to an audio book or classical music or ask someone to read a story to you while you color and draw on the next page.

What are you listening to?

_____

TITLE:

STARS:

Screen Time!

Watch a Documentary, Educational Program, Movie, or Tutorial.

My Review of this Film:

Draw a Scene from the video:

Rating:
AWFUL
BAD
LAME
YUCKY
OKAY
NICE
GOOD
GREAT
SUPER
AMAZING

World News Today!

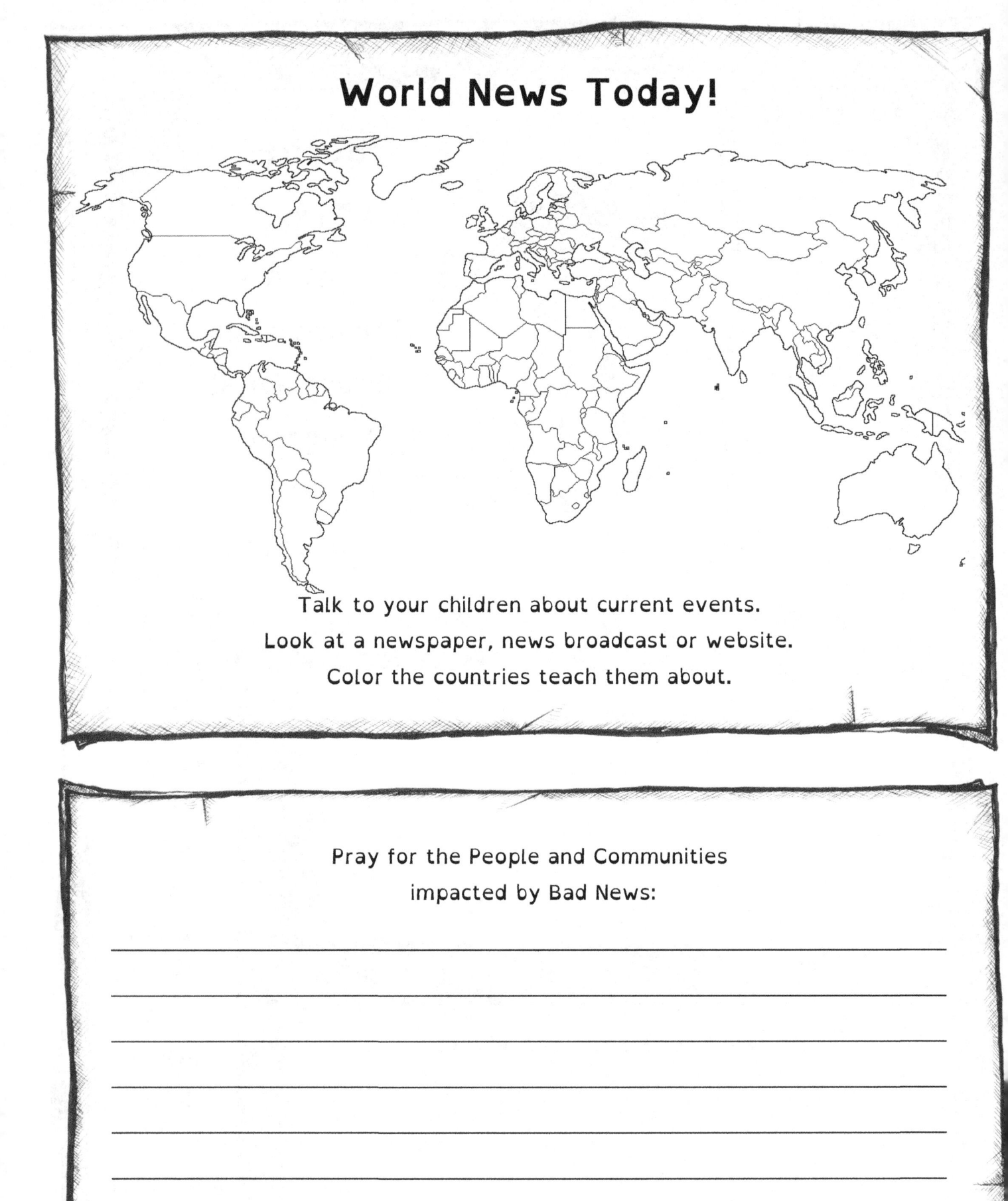

Talk to your children about current events.
Look at a newspaper, news broadcast or website.
Color the countries teach them about.

Pray for the People and Communities
impacted by Bad News:

_____
_____
_____
_____
_____
_____
_____

Daily Journal

_____
_____
_____
_____
_____
_____
_____
_____
_____
_____
_____

"Education is not filling a bucket,
but lighting a fire." ~W.B. Yeats

A New Day!

My Verse, My Song or My Prayer...

_____
_____
_____
_____
_____
_____
_____

What Matters Most...

_____
_____
_____
_____
_____

Prayer List

_____
_____
_____
_____
_____
_____
_____
_____

Reading Time

Sit down with a few books from your stack.

Write, draw or copy the things you want to remember.

Mom's Coloring Time

Coloring beautiful pictures and doodling relieves stress and helps with creativity & relaxation.

"The true sign of intelligence is not knowledge but imagination." ~ Albert Einstein

Plans & Perspective

"The home is the first and most effective place to learn the lessons of life: truth, honor, virtue, self control, the value of education, honest work, and the purpose and privilege of life." - McKay

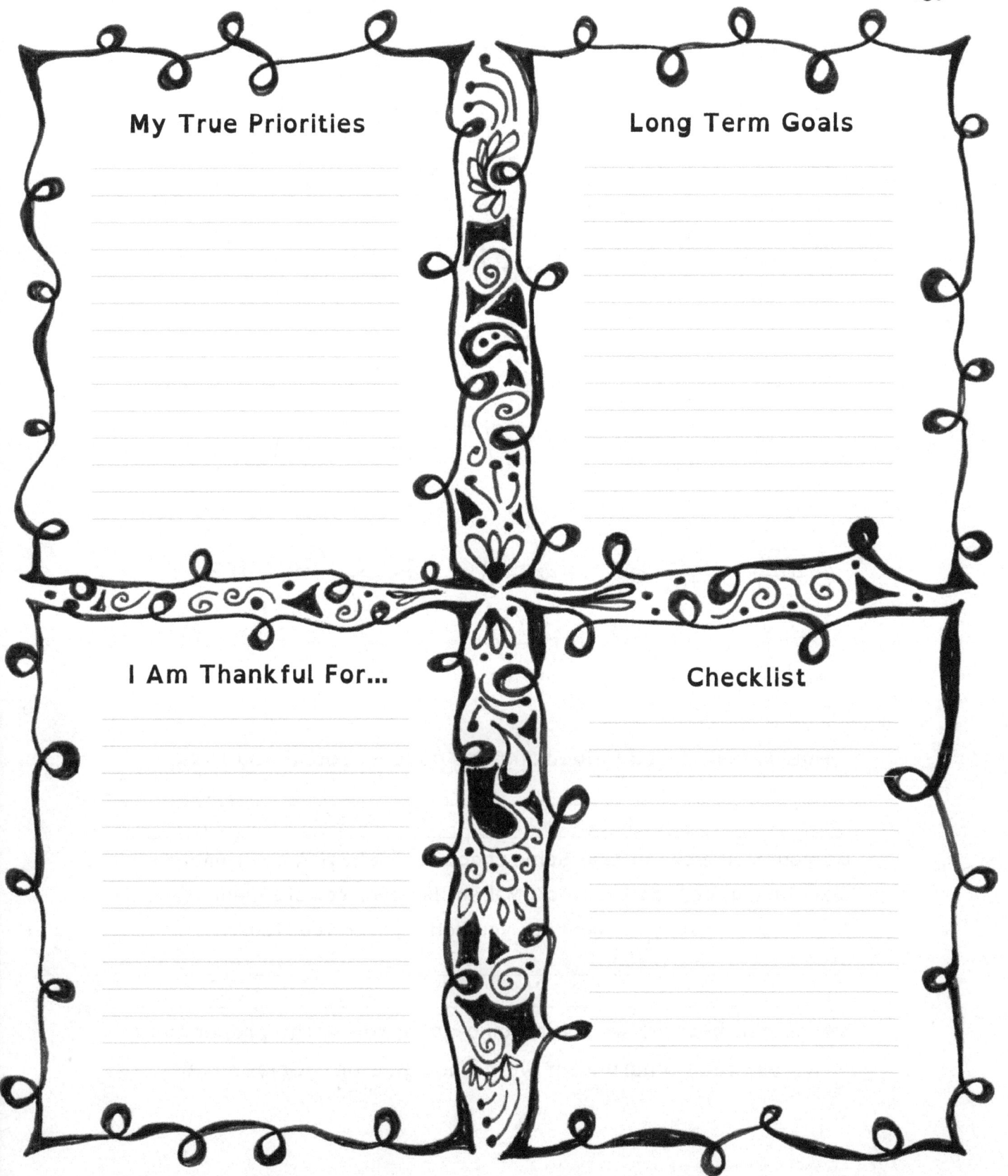

My True Priorities

Long Term Goals

I Am Thankful For...

Checklist

Attitude Improvement Time

How are your feeling today?
Color all the facial expressions that match your day!

| happy | surprised | joy | doubt | distrust |

| self-sufficiency | dreamy | shocked | scared | guile |

| gloomy | engrossment | flash | determination | thoughtful |

| diffidence | offence | confusion | craft | tired |

How is your mood influencing the people around you today?
_____
_____

Do you need a cup of tea? Some chocolate? A hug? A quiet moment? Peaceful music? Stop the clock. Make it happen. You are mom. make a little happy moment for yourself and for your family.
_____
_____

Let us not become weary in doing good, for at the proper time we will reap a harvest if we do not give up. –Galatians 6:9

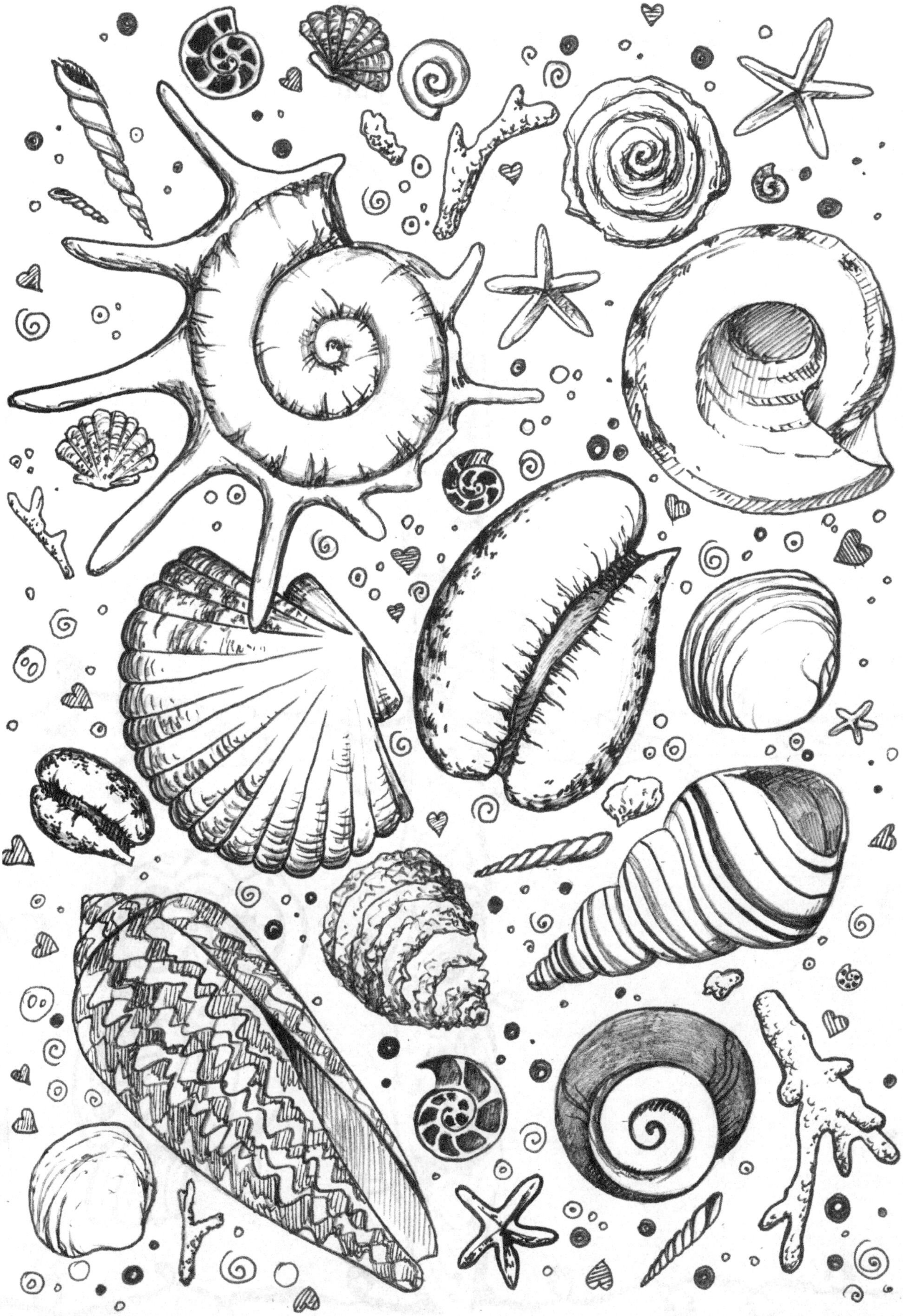

Reading Time

Sit down with a few books from your stack.

Write, draw or copy the things you want to remember.

What song do you want to sing today?
Write a few verses here:

Mom's Illustrated TO-DO List

Ideas for Fun & Learning Together

Menu Planning
Open up an old-fashion cookbook!

_____
_____
_____
_____
_____
_____

Shopping List

_____
_____
_____
_____
_____
_____
_____
_____
_____

Draw a Meal PLAN

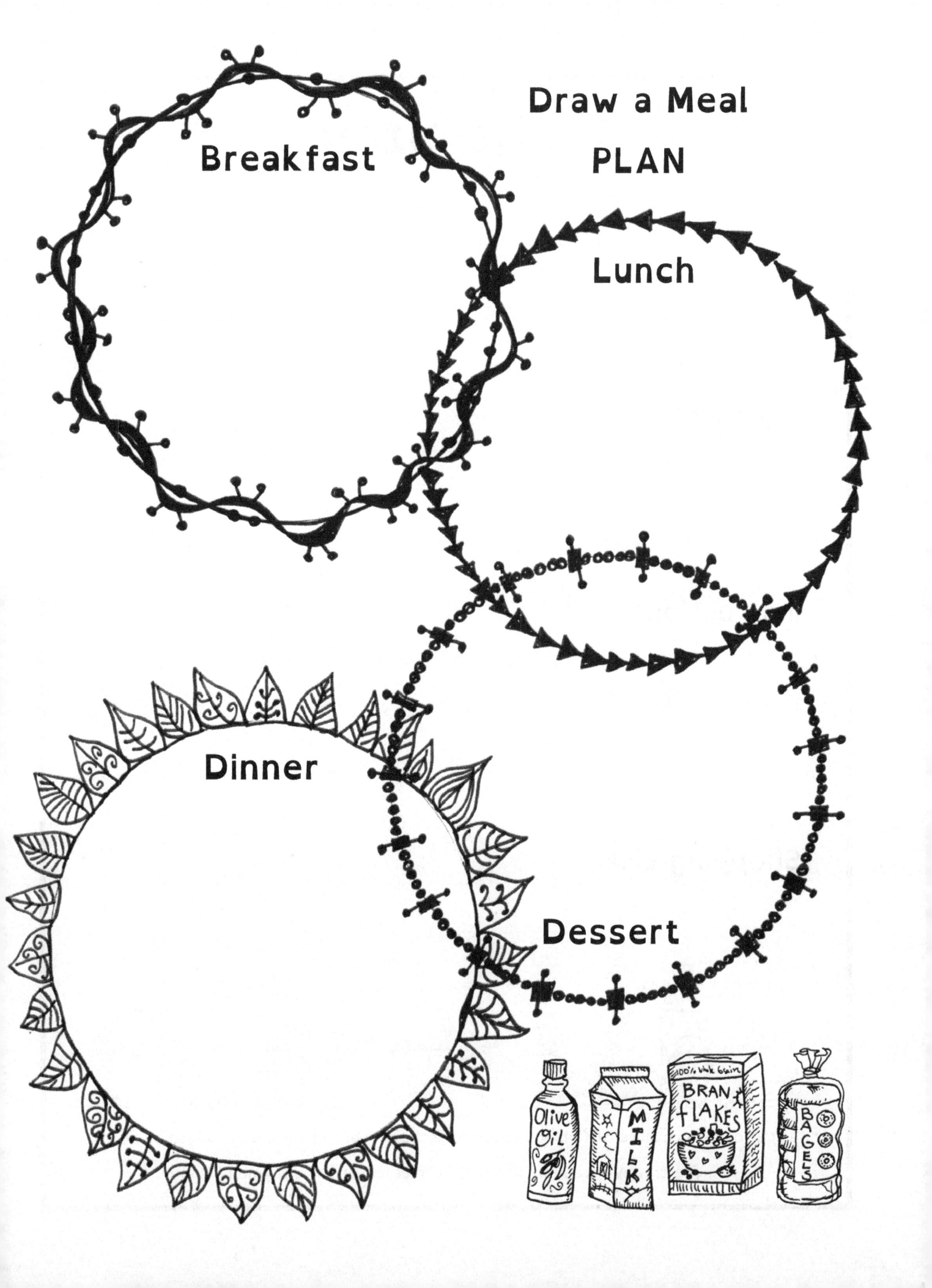

Breakfast

Lunch

Dinner

Dessert

Recipe:

_____

Serves:

Prep Time:

Ingredients:

Instructions:

Shopping List:

"Recipe for genius: More of family and less of school, more of parents and less of peers, more creative freedom and less formal lessons." ~Raymond Moore

Reading Time

Sit down with a few books from your stack.

Write, draw or copy the things you want to remember.

Mommy Math Time

Math is something that Kids need help with.
Go get a kid and show them how to do some math here:

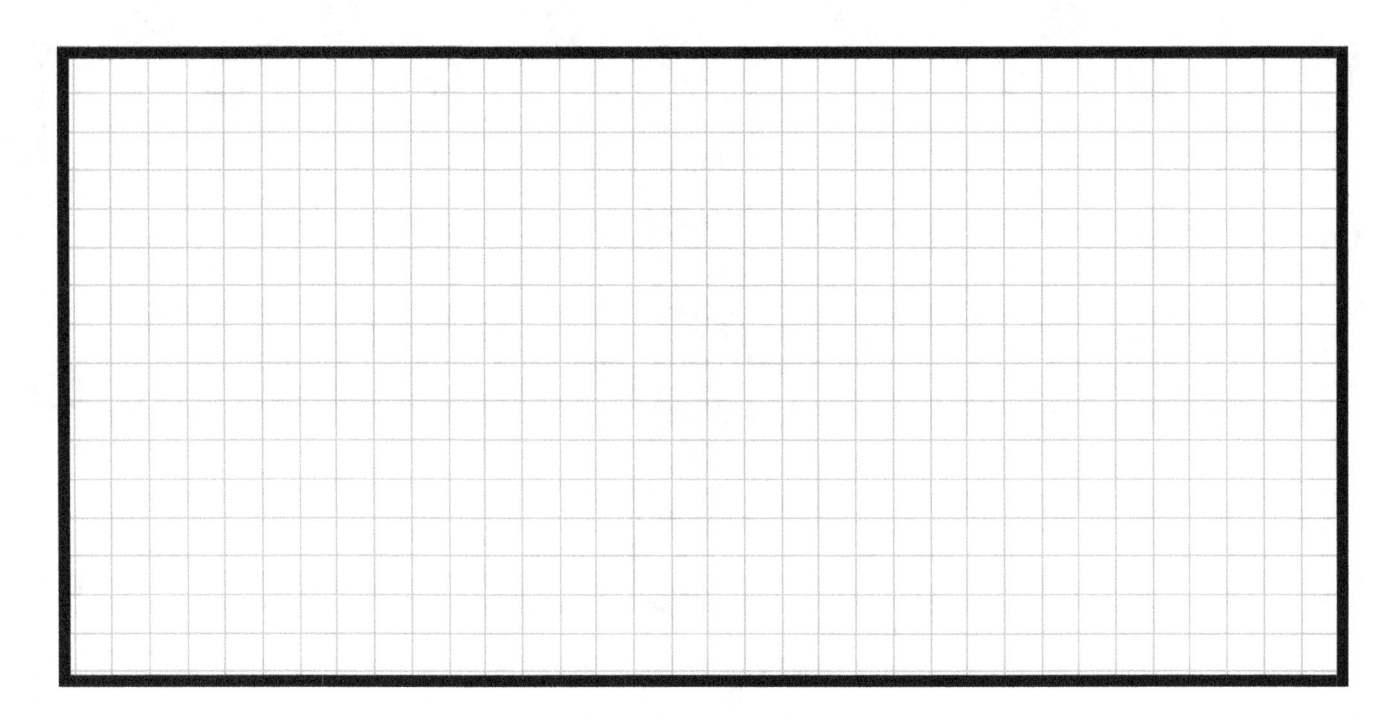

"Everything I am interested in, from cooking to electronics, is related to math. In real life you don't have to worry about integrating math into other subjects. In real life, math already is integrated into everything else." ~ Hoffstrom

Listening Time

Listen to an audio book or classical music or ask someone to read a story to you while you color and draw on the next page.

What are you listening to?

_____

TITLE:

STARS:

Screen Time!

Watch a Documentary, Educational Program, Movie, or Tutorial.

My Review of this Film:

Draw a Scene from the video:

Rating:
AWFUL
BAD
LAME
YUCKY
OKAY
NICE
GOOD
GREAT
SUPER
AMAZING

World News Today!

Talk to your children about current events.
Look at a newspaper, news broadcast or website.
Color the countries teach them about.

Pray for the People and Communities
impacted by Bad News:

_____
_____
_____
_____
_____
_____
_____

Daily Journal

_____
_____
_____
_____
_____
_____
_____
_____
_____
_____

"Education is not filling a bucket,
but lighting a fire." ~W.B. Yeats

Special Memories

Things that you want to remember...

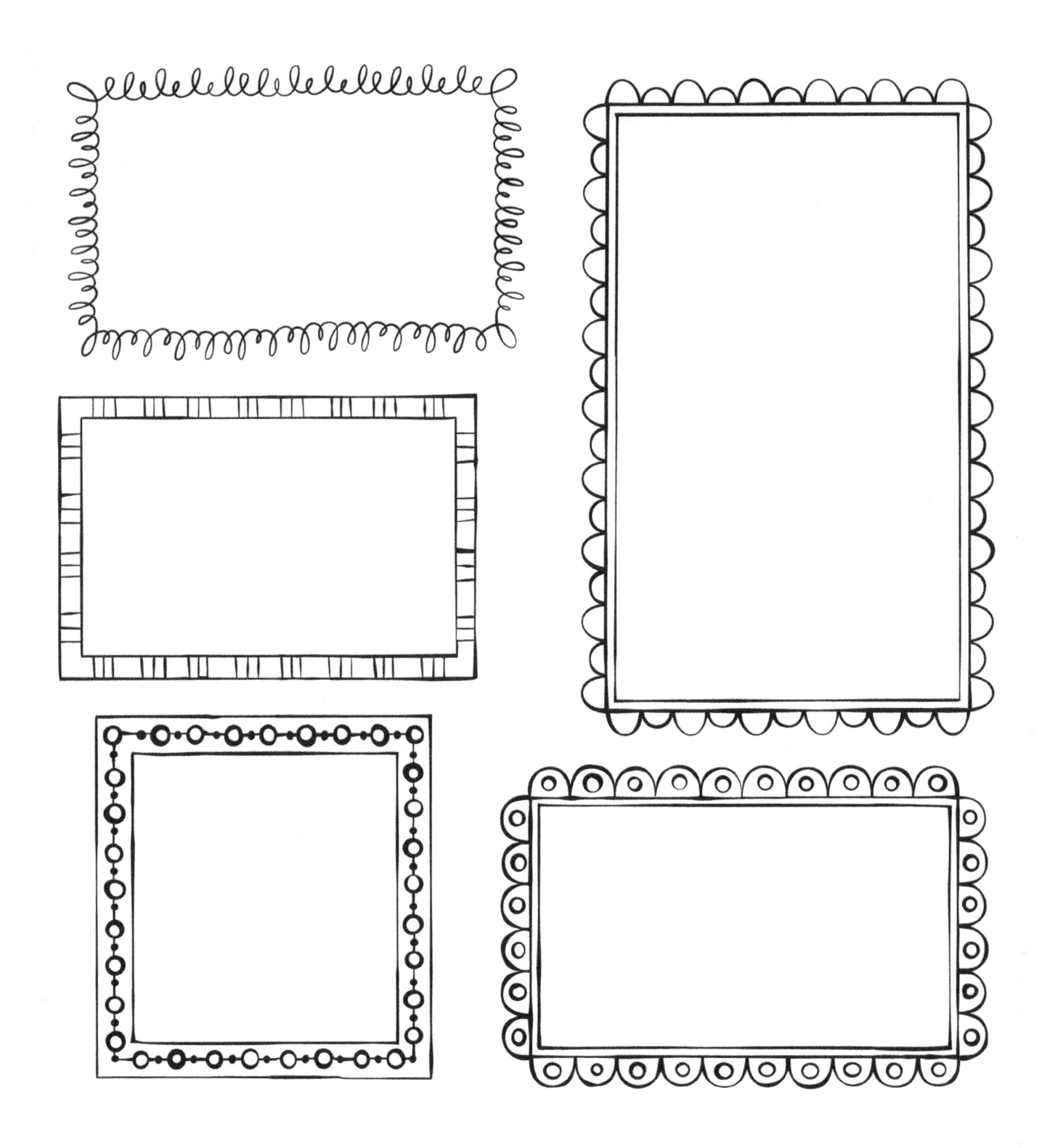

A New Day!

My Verse, My Song or My Prayer...
_____
_____
_____
_____
_____
_____

What Matters Most...
_____
_____
_____
_____
_____

Prayer List
_____
_____
_____
_____
_____
_____
_____
_____

Mom's Coloring Time

Coloring beautiful pictures and doodling relieves stress and helps with creativity & relaxation.

GIVING LIGHT

"The true sign of intelligence is not knowledge but imagination." ~ Albert Einstein

Reading Time

Sit down with a few books from your stack.

Write, draw or copy the things you want to remember.

Plans & Perspective

"The home is the first and most effective place to learn the lessons of life: truth, honor, virtue, self control, the value of education, honest work, and the purpose and privilege of life." - McKay

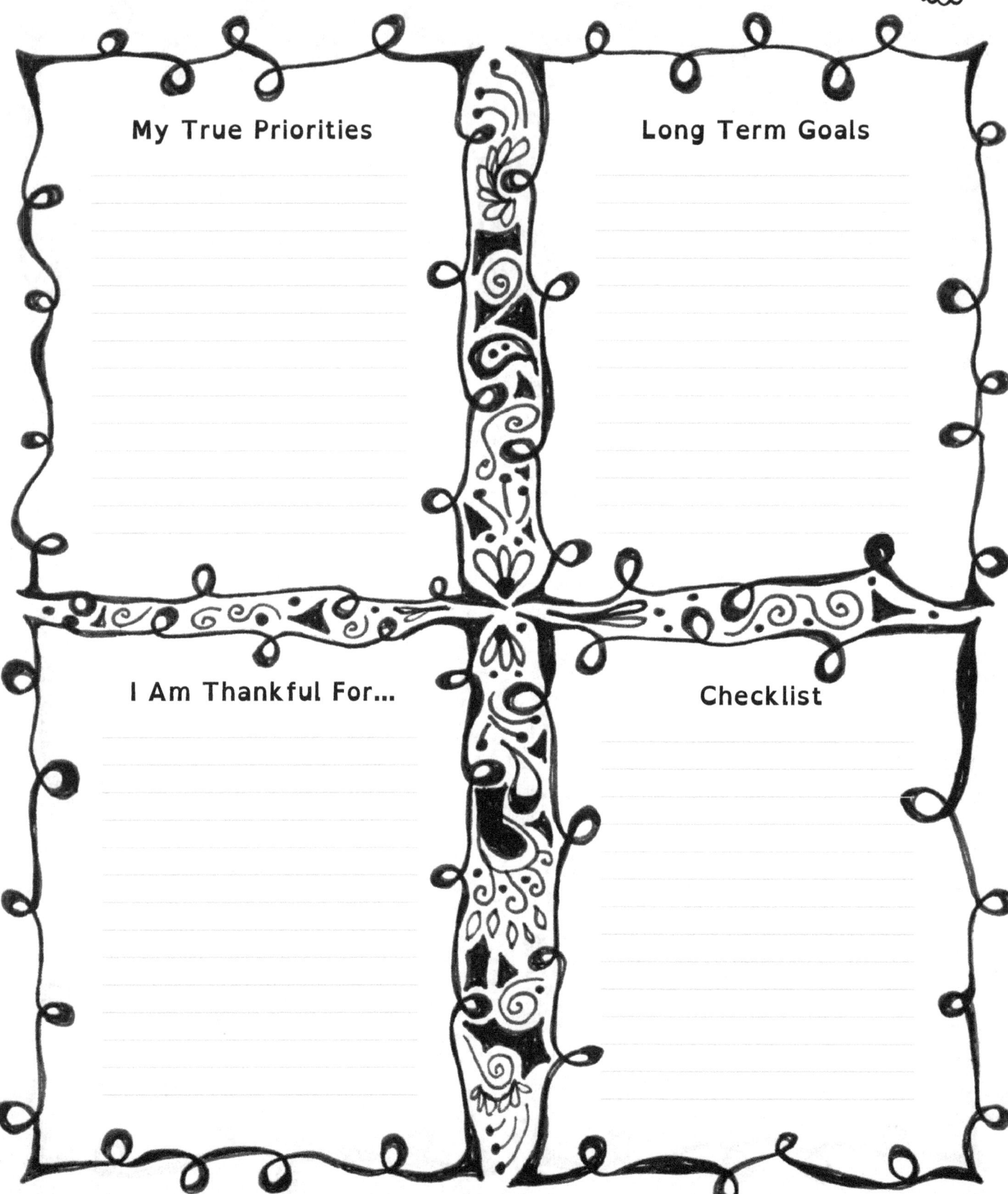

My True Priorities

Long Term Goals

I Am Thankful For...

Checklist

A New Day!

My Verse, My Song or My Prayer...

What Matters Most...

Prayer List

Mom's Coloring Time

Coloring beautiful pictures and doodling relieves stress and helps with creativity & relaxation.

"The true sign of intelligence is not knowledge but imagination." ~ Albert Einstein

Plans & Perspective

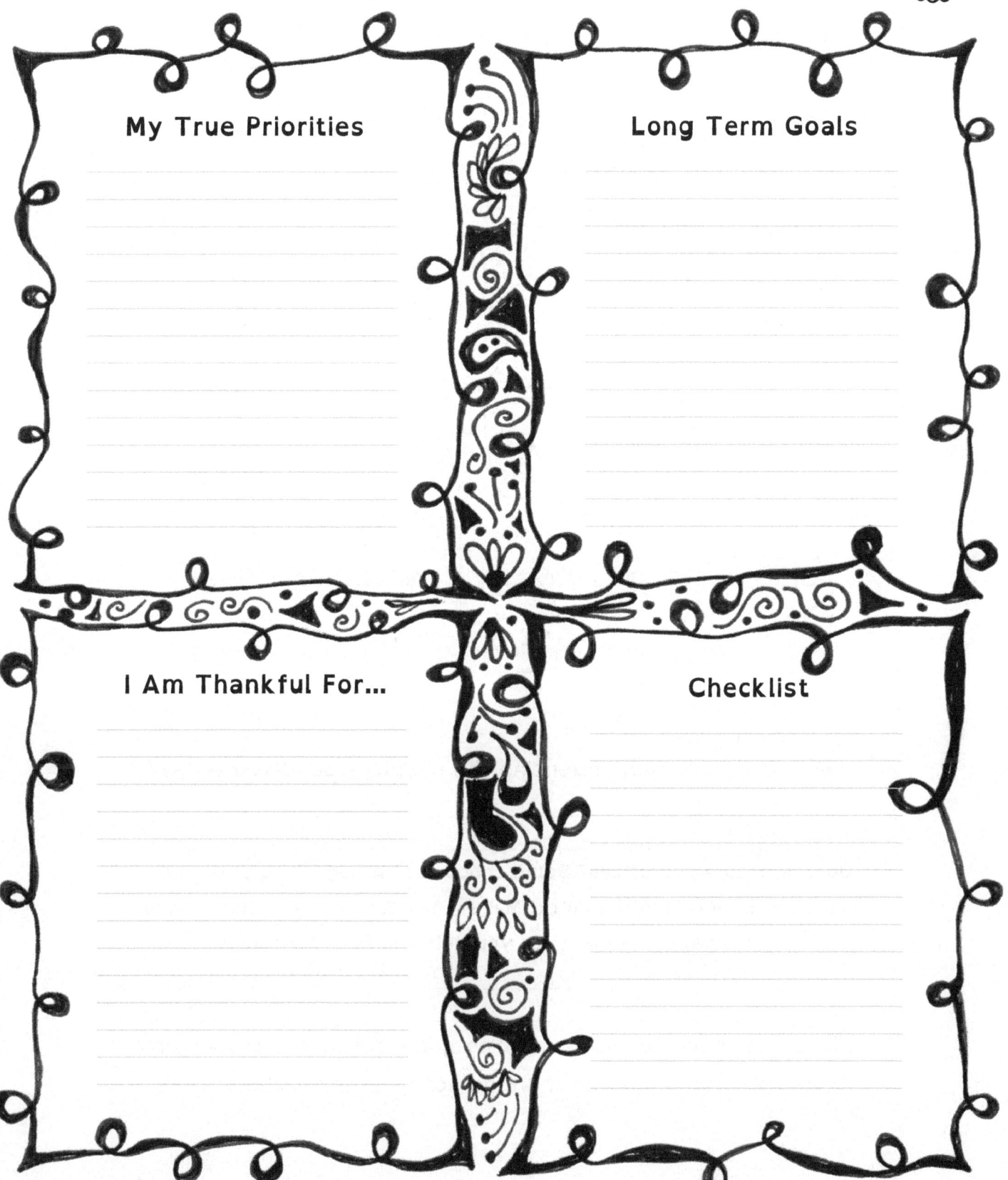

"The home is the first and most effective place to learn the lessons of life: truth, honor, virtue, self control, the value of education, honest work, and the purpose and privilege of life." - McKay

My True Priorities

Long Term Goals

I Am Thankful For...

Checklist

Attitude Improvement Time

How are your feeling today?
Color all the facial expressions that match your day!

happy	surprised	joy	doubt	distrust
self-sufficiency	dreamy	shocked	scared	guile
gloomy	engrossment	flash	determination	thoughtful
diffidence	offence	confusion	craft	tired

How is your mood influencing the people around you today?
_____
_____

Do you need a cup of tea? Some chocolate? A hug? A quiet moment? Peaceful music? Stop the clock. Make it happen. You are mom. make a little happy moment for yourself and for your family.
_____
_____

Let us not become weary in doing good, for at the proper time we will reap a harvest if we do not give up. –Galatians 6:9

Reading Time

Sit down with a few books from your stack.

Write, draw or copy the things you want to remember.

What song do you want to sing today?
Write a few verses here:

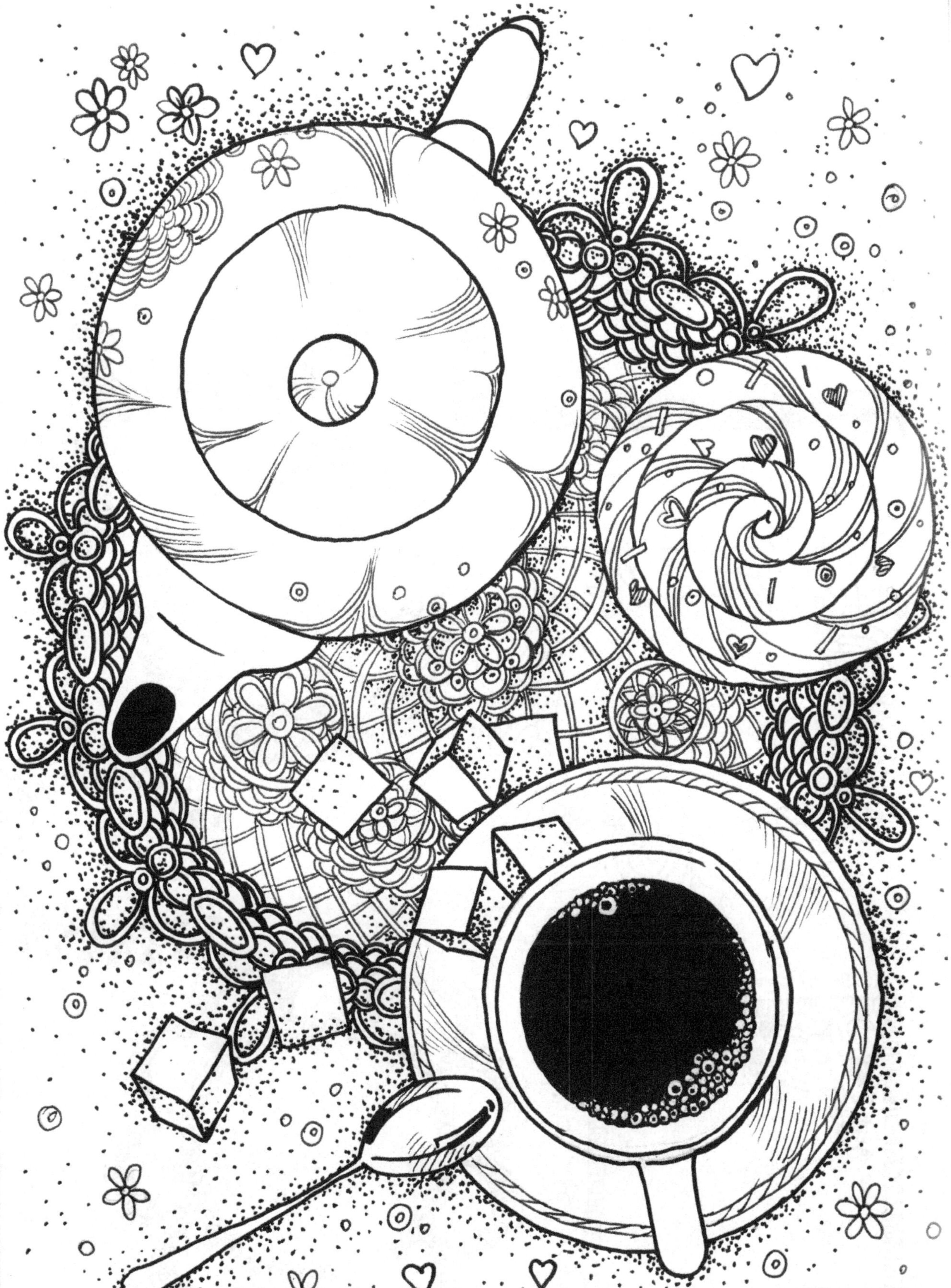

Mom's Illustrated TO-DO List

Ideas for Fun & Learning Together

Menu Planning

Open up an old-fashion cookbook!

_____
_____
_____
_____
_____
_____

Shopping List

_____
_____
_____
_____
_____
_____
_____
_____

Reading Time

Sit down with a few books from your stack.

Write, draw or copy the things you want to remember.

Draw a Meal PLAN

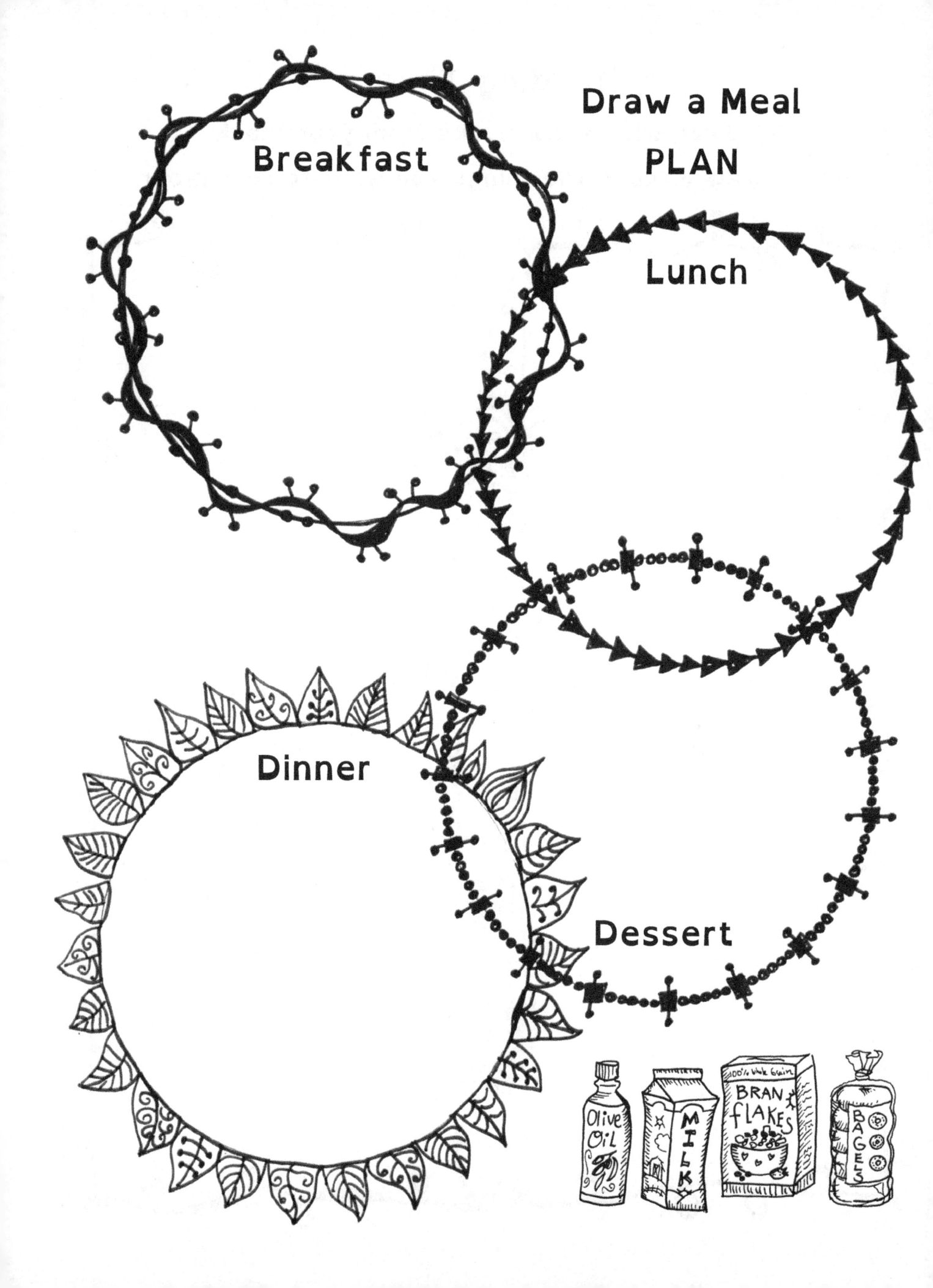

- Breakfast
- Lunch
- Dinner
- Dessert

Recipe:

_____

Serves:

Prep Time:

Ingredients:

Instructions:

Shopping List:

"Recipe for genius: More of family and less of school, more of parents and less of peers, more creative freedom and less formal lessons." ~Raymond Moore

Mommy Math Time

Math is something that Kids need help with.
Go get a kid and show them how to do some math here:

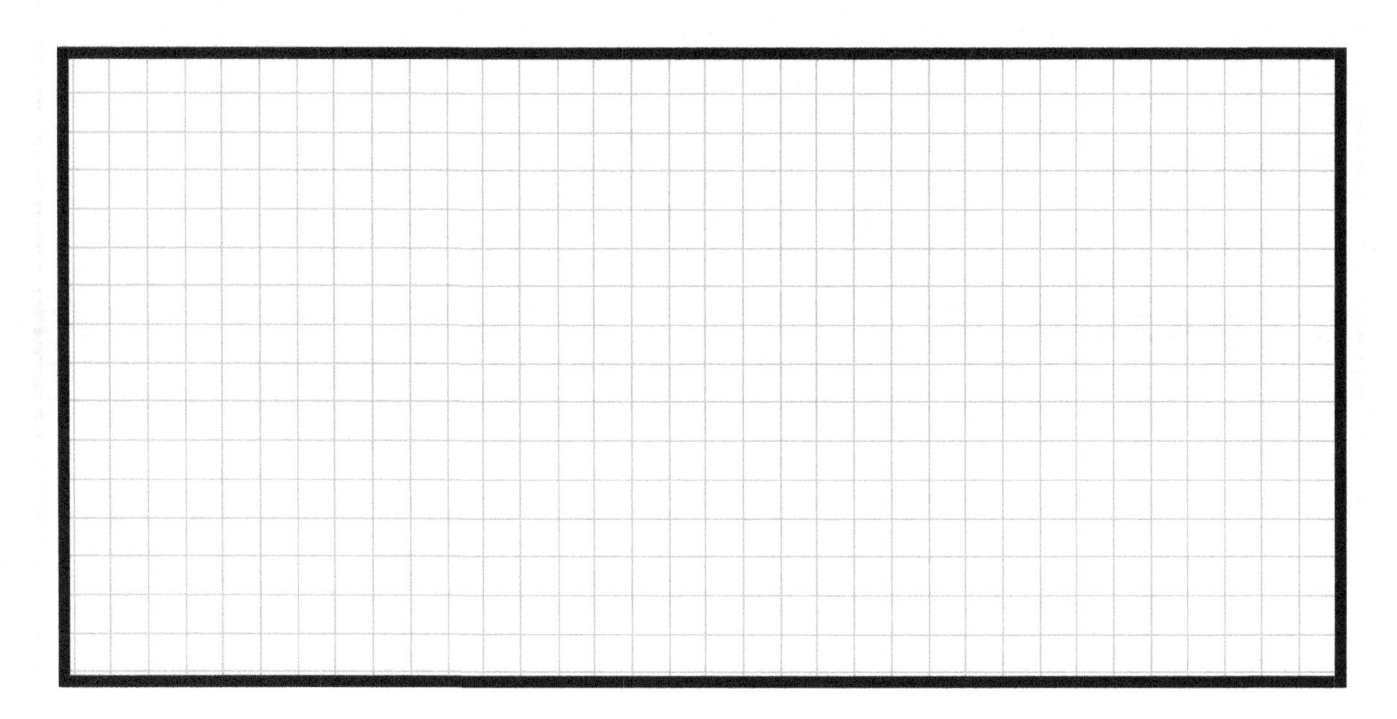

"Everything I am interested in, from cooking to electronics, is related to math. In real life you don't have to worry about integrating math into other subjects. In real life, math already is integrated into everything else." ~ Hoffstrom

Listening Time

Listen to an audio book or classical music or ask someone to read a story to you while you color and draw on the next page.

What are you listening to?

_____

TITLE:

STARS:

Screen Time!

Watch a Documentary, Educational Program, Movie, or Tutorial.

My Review of this Film:

Draw a Scene from the video:

Rating:
AWFUL
BAD
LAME
YUCKY
OKAY
NICE
GOOD
GREAT
SUPER
AMAZING

World News Today!

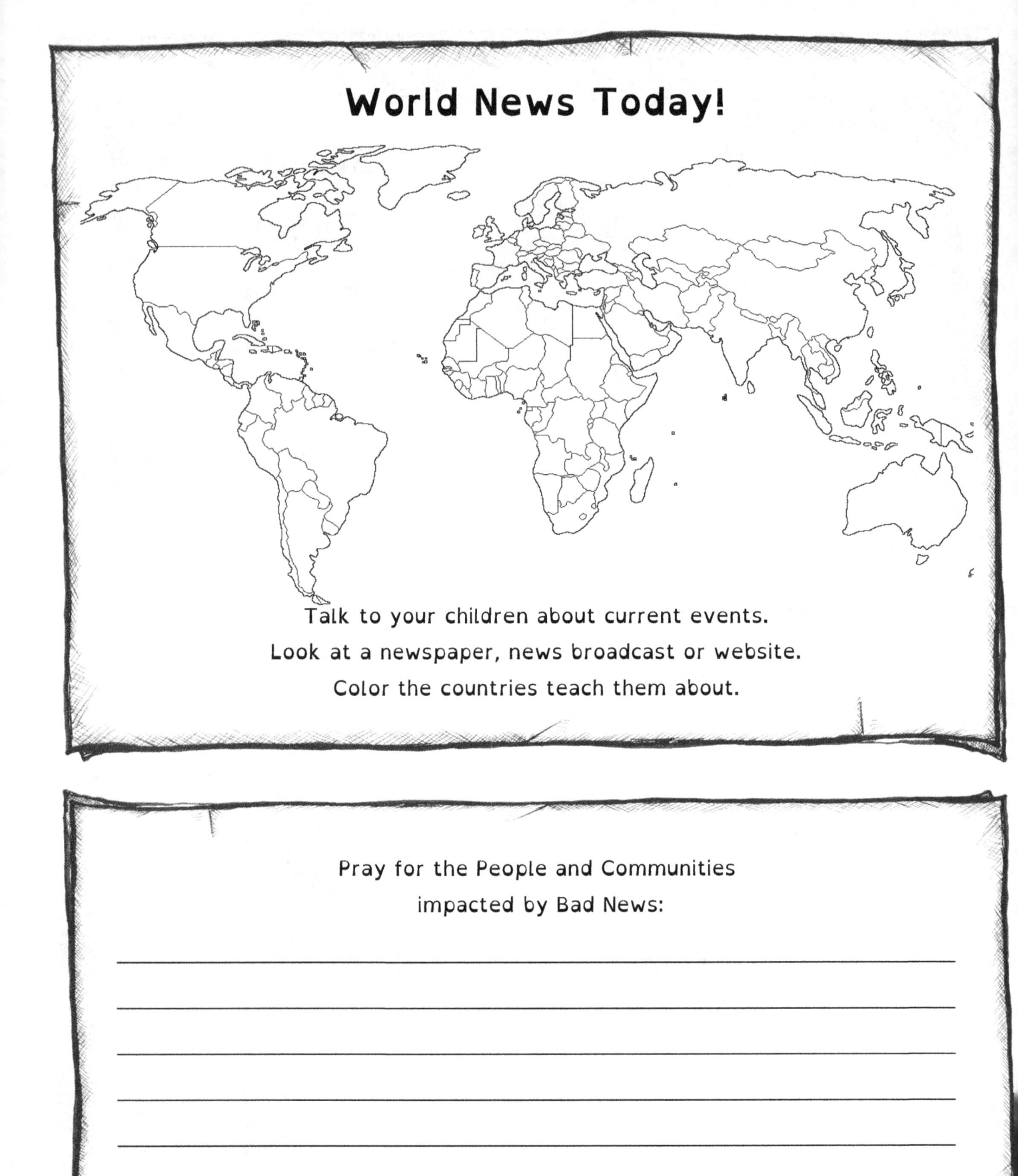

Talk to your children about current events.
Look at a newspaper, news broadcast or website.
Color the countries teach them about.

Pray for the People and Communities
impacted by Bad News:

_____
_____
_____
_____
_____
_____
_____

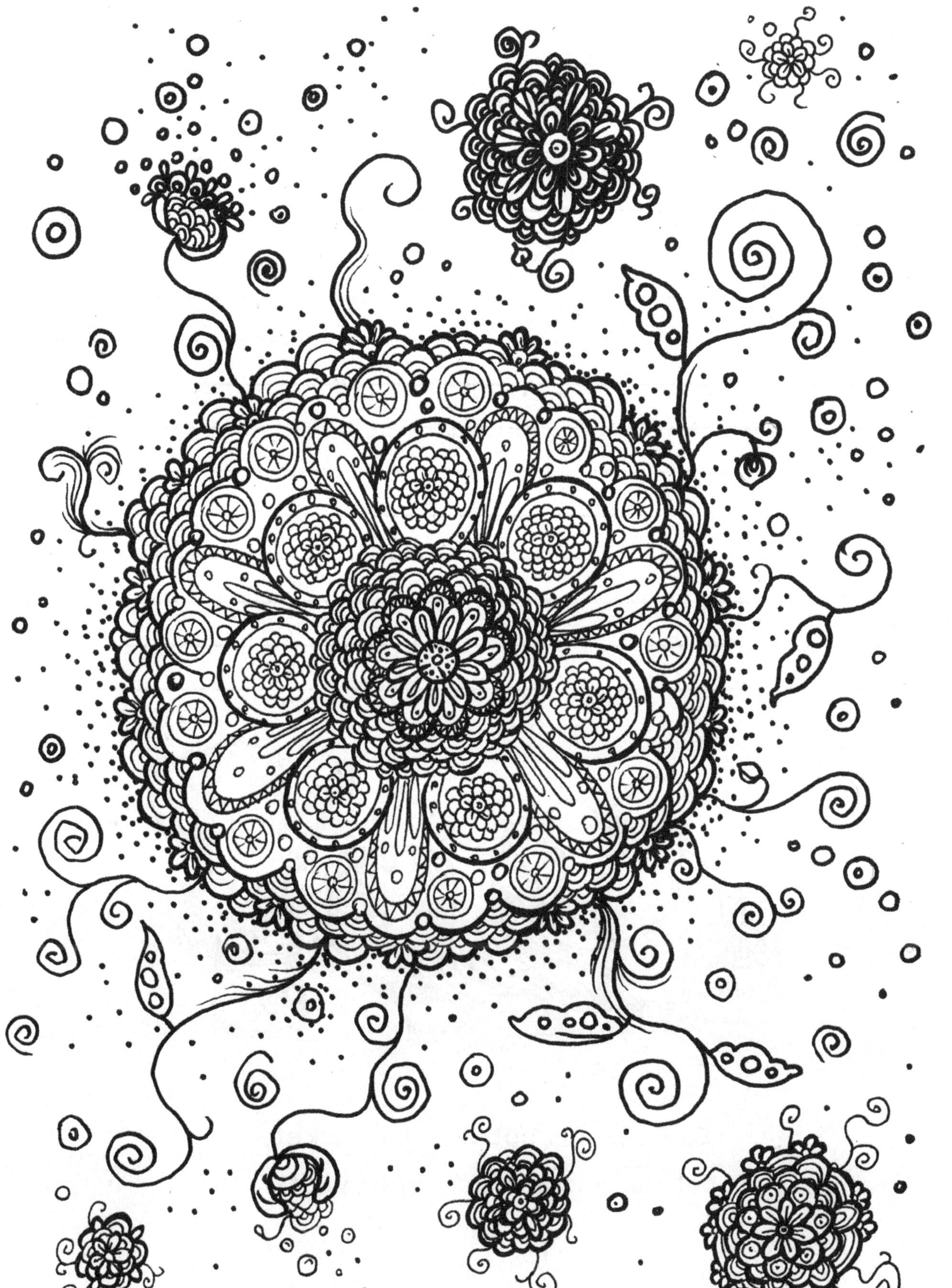

Daily Journal

_____
_____
_____
_____
_____
_____
_____
_____
_____
_____

"Education is not filling a bucket,
but lighting a fire." ~W.B. Yeats

Special Memories
Things that you want to remember...

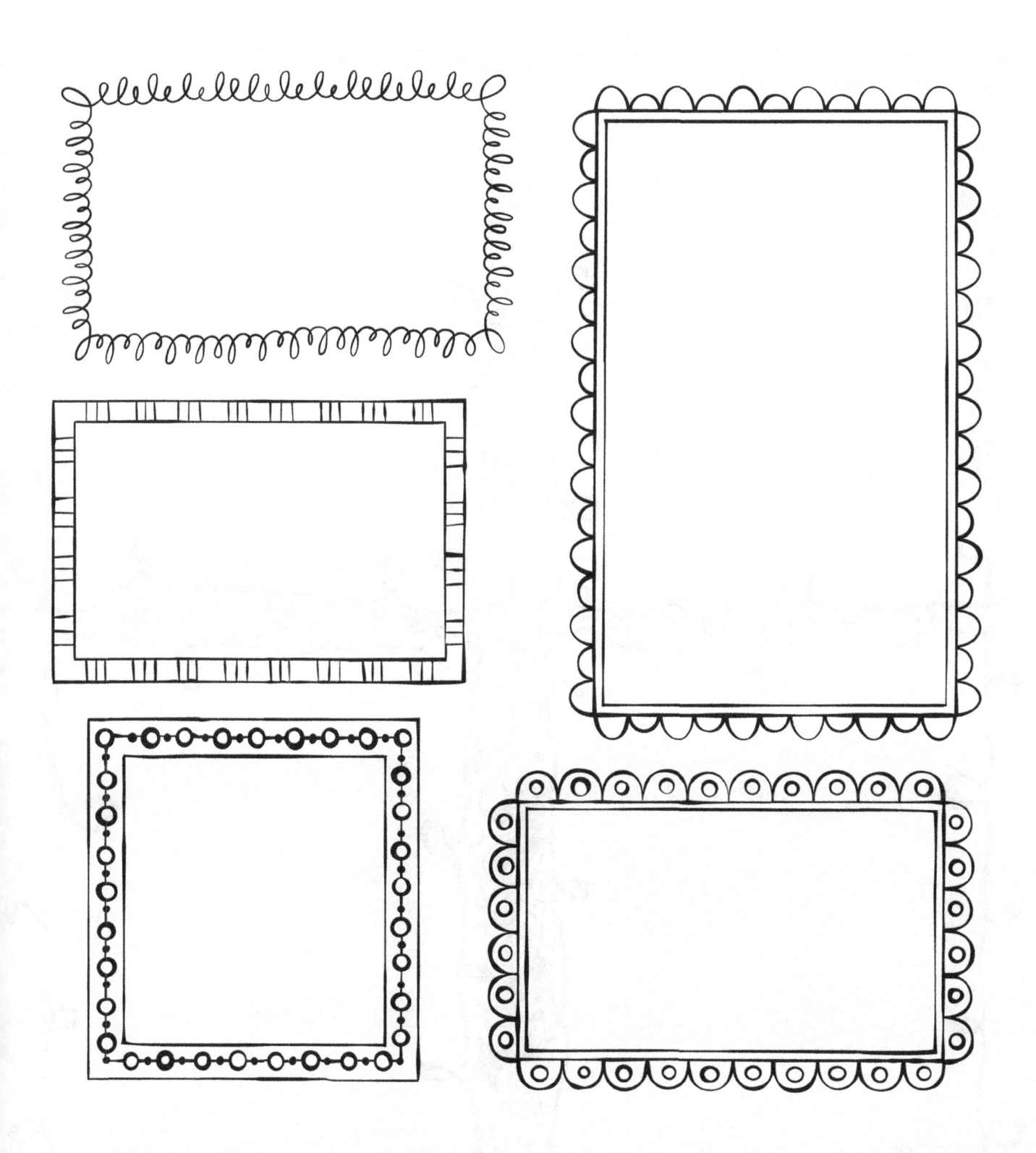

Reading Time

Sit down with a few books from your stack.

Write, draw or copy the things you want to remember.

A New Day!

My Verse, My Song or My Prayer...

_____
_____
_____
_____
_____
_____

What Matters Most...

_____
_____
_____
_____
_____

Prayer List

_____
_____
_____
_____
_____
_____
_____
_____

Mom's Coloring Time

Coloring beautiful pictures and doodling relieves stress and helps with creativity & relaxation.

"The true sign of intelligence is not knowledge but imagination." ~ Albert Einstein

Plans & Perspective

"The home is the first and most effective place to learn the lessons of life: truth, honor, virtue, self control, the value of education, honest work, and the purpose and privilege of life." - McKay

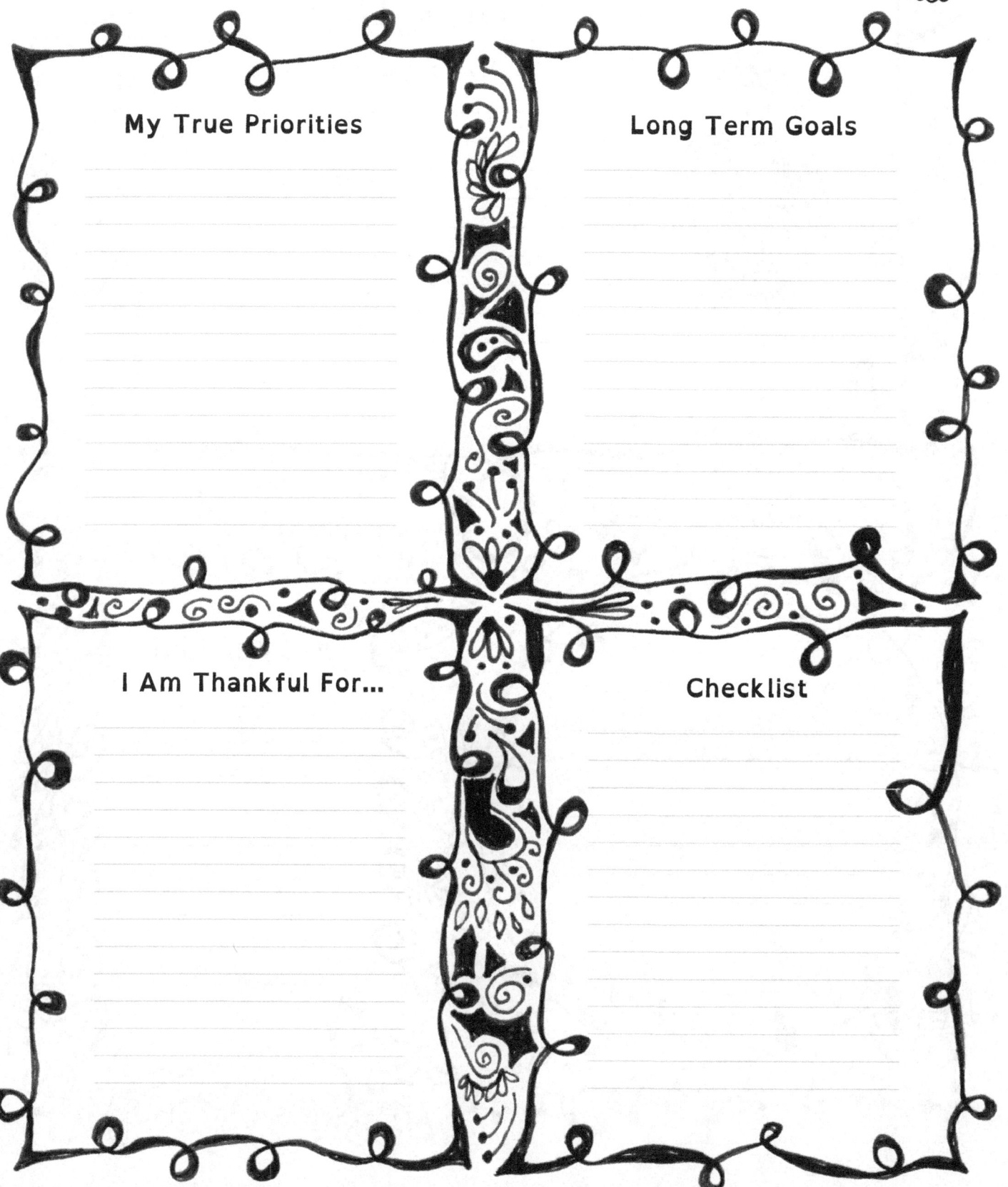

My True Priorities

Long Term Goals

I Am Thankful For...

Checklist

A New Day!

My Verse, My Song or My Prayer...

_____
_____
_____
_____
_____
_____
_____

What Matters Most...

_____
_____
_____
_____
_____

Prayer List

_____
_____
_____
_____
_____
_____
_____

Mom's Coloring Time

Coloring beautiful pictures and doodling relieves stress and helps with creativity & relaxation.

"The true sign of intelligence is not knowledge but imagination." ~ Albert Einstein

Plans & Perspective

"The home is the first and most effective place to learn the lessons of life: truth, honor, virtue, self control, the value of education, honest work, and the purpose and privilege of life." - McKay

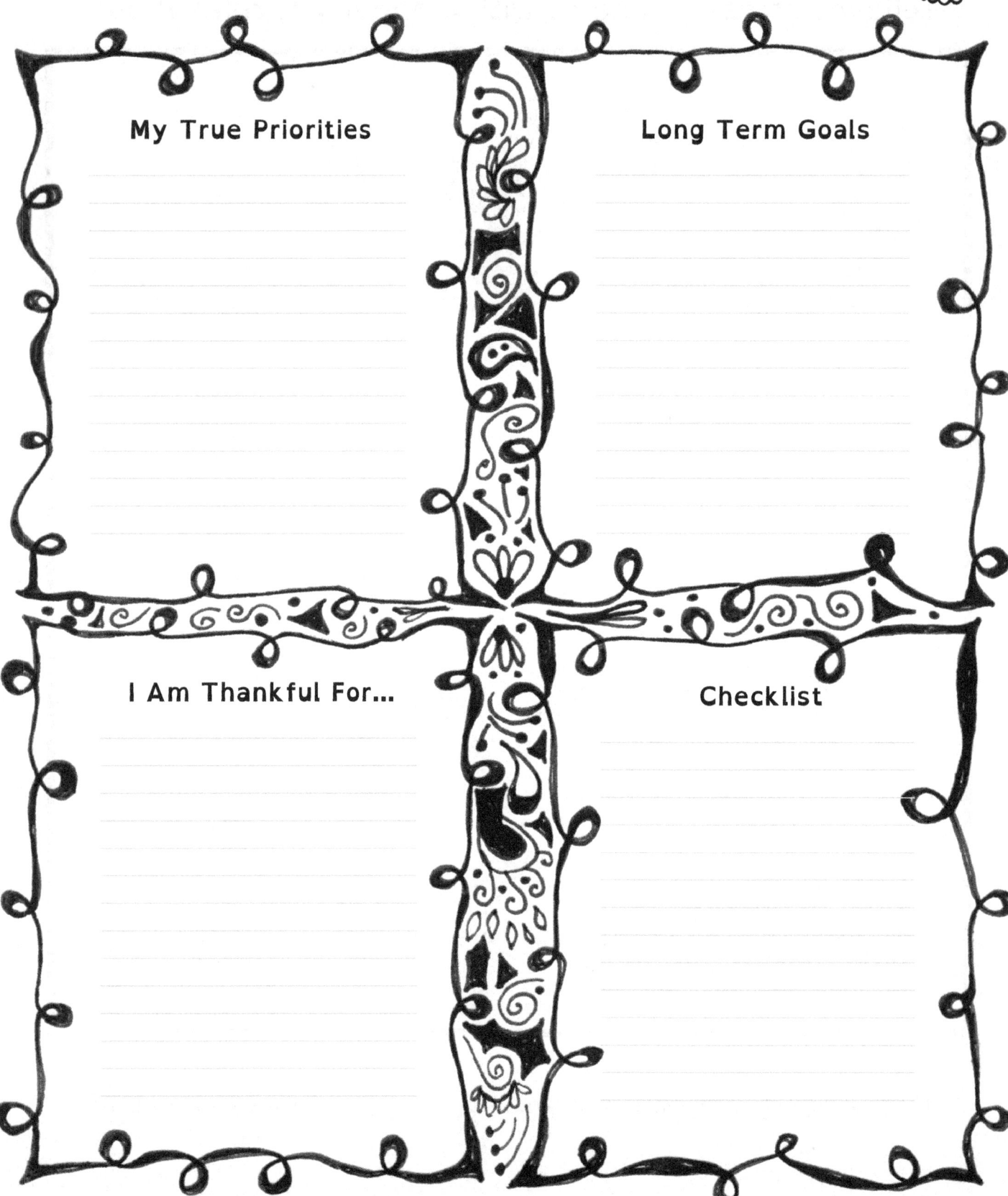

My True Priorities

Long Term Goals

I Am Thankful For...

Checklist

Attitude Improvement Time

How are your feeling today?
Color all the facial expressions that match your day!

| happy | surprised | joy | doubt | distrust |

| self-sufficiency | dreamy | shocked | scared | guile |

| gloomy | engrossment | flash | determination | thoughtful |

| diffidence | offence | confusion | craft | tired |

How is your mood influencing the people around you today?
_____
_____

Do you need a cup of tea? Some chocolate? A hug? A quiet moment? Peaceful music? Stop the clock. Make it happen. You are mom. make a little happy moment for yourself and for your family.
_____
_____

Let us not become weary in doing good, for at the proper time we will reap a harvest if we do not give up. –Galatians 6:9

Reading Time

Sit down with a few books from your stack.

Write, draw or copy the things you want to remember.

Mom's Illustrated TO-DO List

Reading Time

Sit down with a few books from your stack.

Write, draw or copy the things you want to remember.

Ideas for Fun & Learning Together

Menu Planning

Open up an old-fashion cookbook!

_____
_____
_____
_____
_____
_____

Shopping List

_____
_____
_____
_____
_____
_____
_____
_____
_____

Draw a Meal PLAN

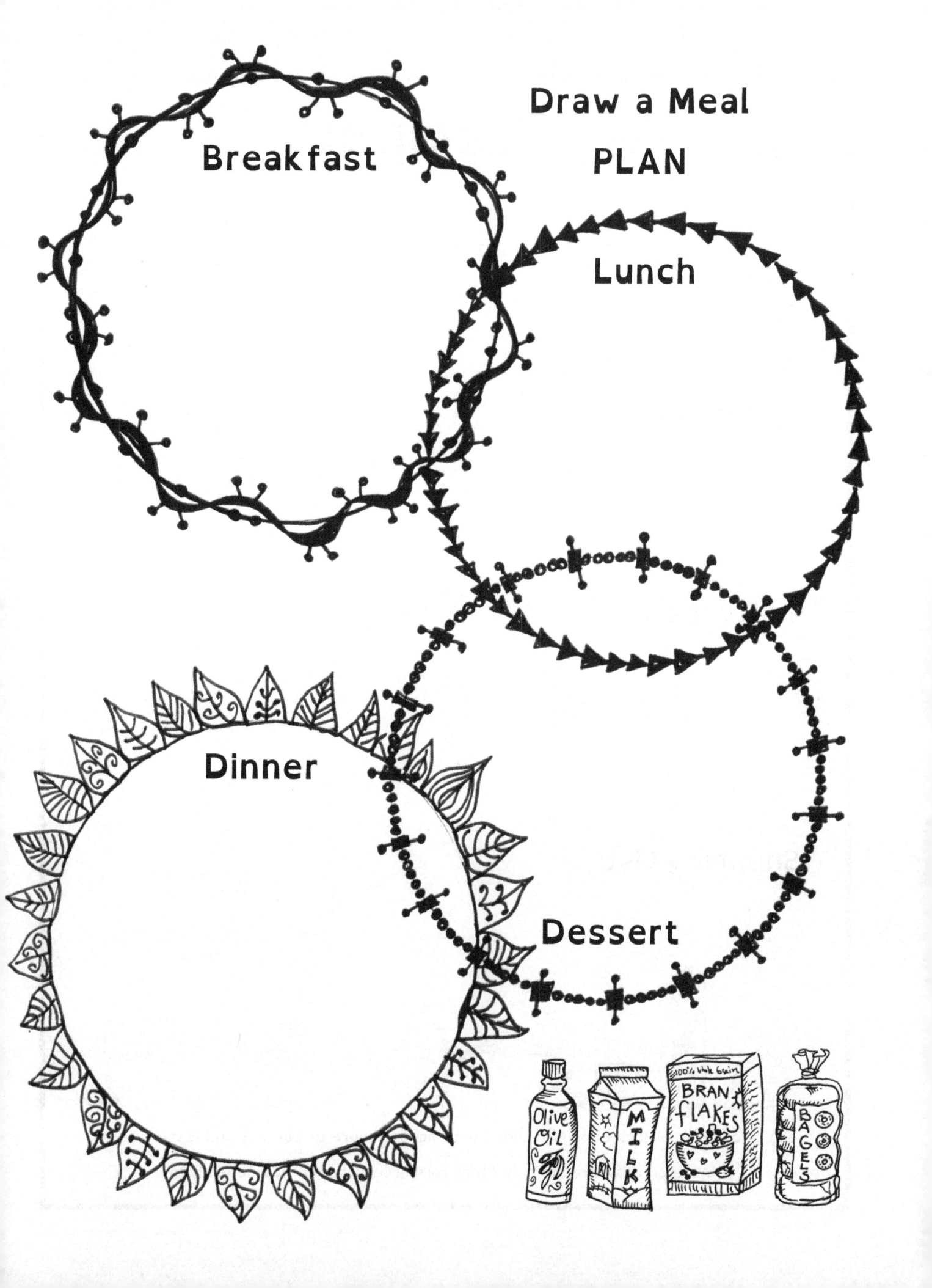

- Breakfast
- Lunch
- Dinner
- Dessert

Recipe:

_____

Serves:

Prep Time:

Ingredients:

Instructions:

Shopping List:

"Recipe for genius: More of family and less of school, more of parents and less of peers, more creative freedom and less formal lessons." ~Raymond Moore

What song do you want to sing today?
Write a few verses here:

Mommy Math Time

Math is something that Kids need help with.
Go get a kid and show them how to do some math here:

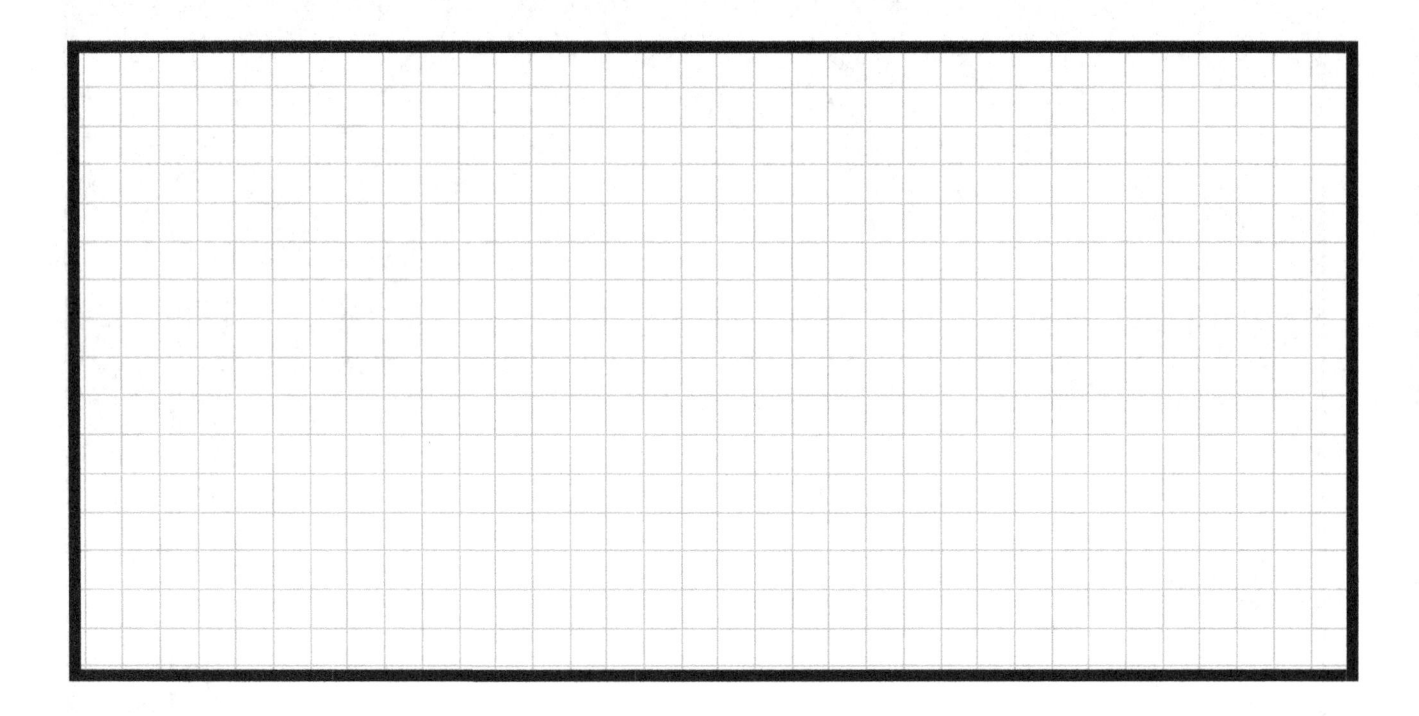

"Everything I am interested in, from cooking to electronics, is related to math. In real life you don't have to worry about integrating math into other subjects. In real life, math already is integrated into everything else." ~ Hoffstrom

Listening Time

Listen to an audio book or classical music or ask someone to read a story to you while you color and draw on the next page.

What are you listening to?

_____

TITLE:

STARS:

Screen Time!

Watch a Documentary, Educational Program, Movie, or Tutorial.

My Review of this Film:

Rating:
AWFUL
BAD
LAME
YUCKY
OKAY
NICE
GOOD
GREAT
SUPER
AMAZING

Draw a Scene from the video:

World News Today!

Talk to your children about current events.
Look at a newspaper, news broadcast or website.
Color the countries teach them about.

Pray for the People and Communities
impacted by Bad News:

_____
_____
_____
_____
_____
_____
_____

Daily Journal

_____
_____
_____
_____
_____
_____
_____
_____
_____
_____

"Education is not filling a bucket,
but lighting a fire." ~W.B. Yeats

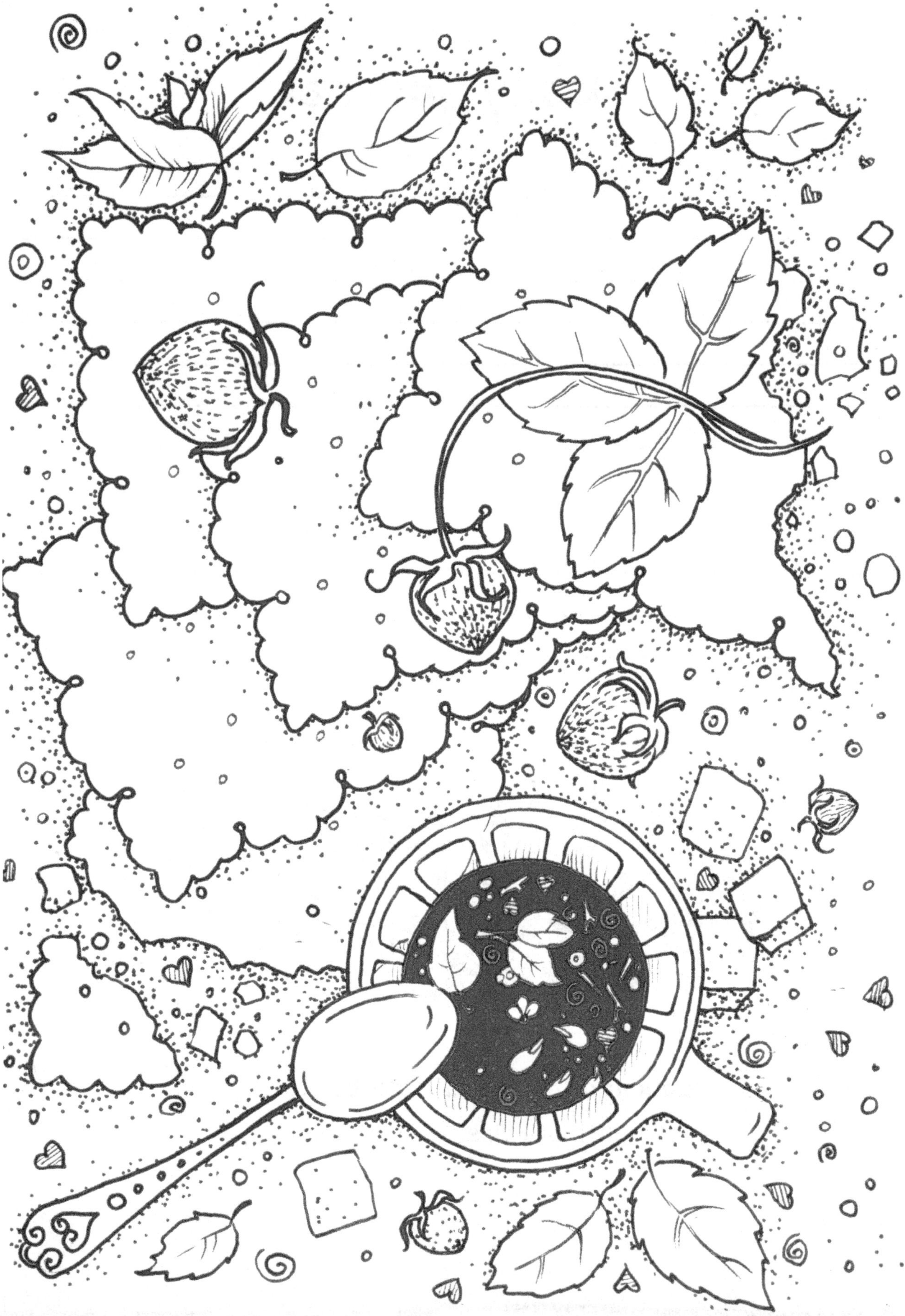

Reading Time

Sit down with a few books from your stack.

Write, draw or copy the things you want to remember.

Special Memories

Things that you want to remember...

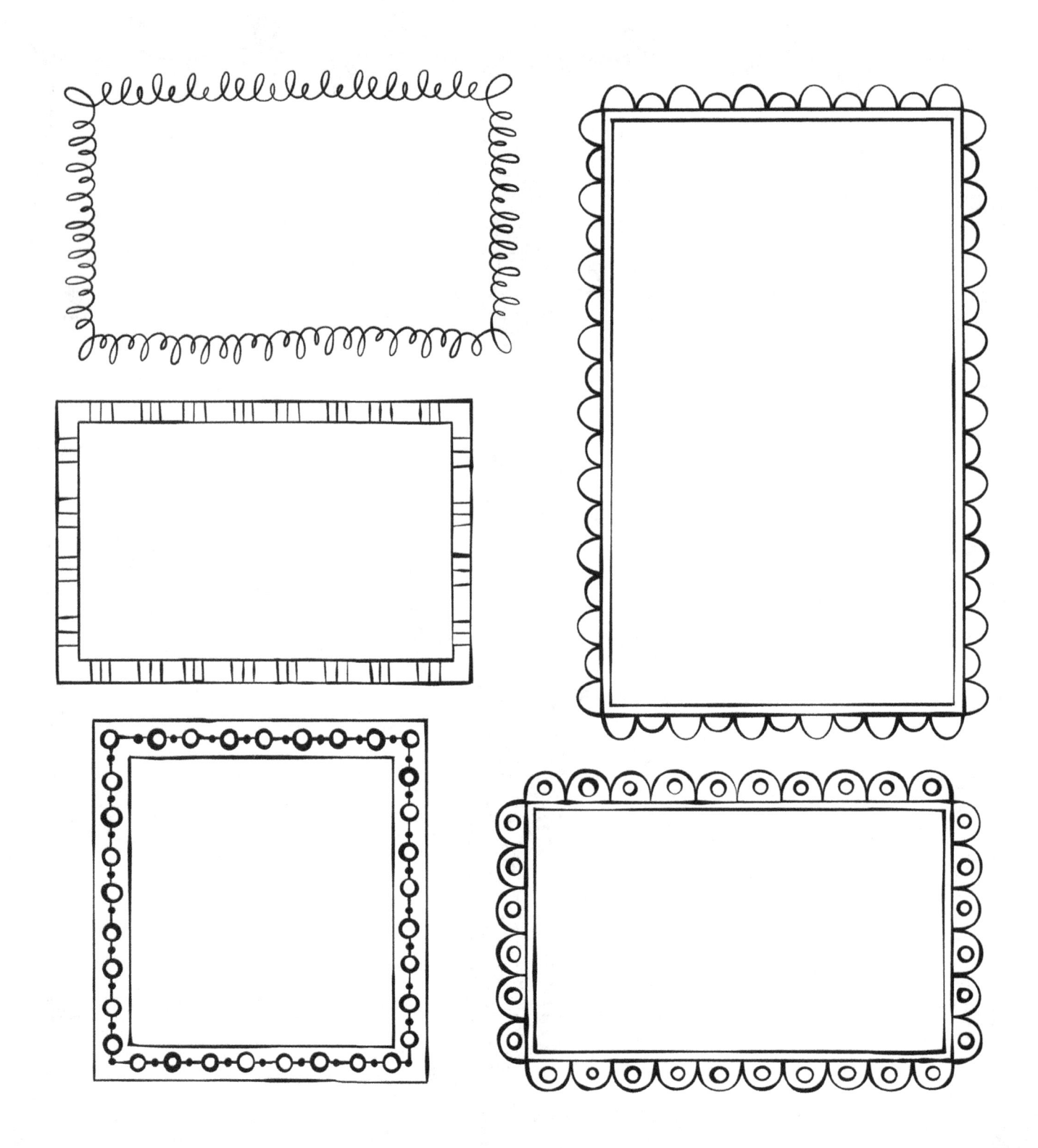

A New Day!

My Verse, My Song or My Prayer...

What Matters Most...

Prayer List

Mom's Coloring Time

Coloring beautiful pictures and doodling relieves stress and helps with creativity & relaxation.

"The true sign of intelligence is not knowledge but imagination." ~ Albert Einstein

Plans & Perspective

"The home is the first and most effective place to learn the lessons of life: truth, honor, virtue, self control, the value of education, honest work, and the purpose and privilege of life." - McKay

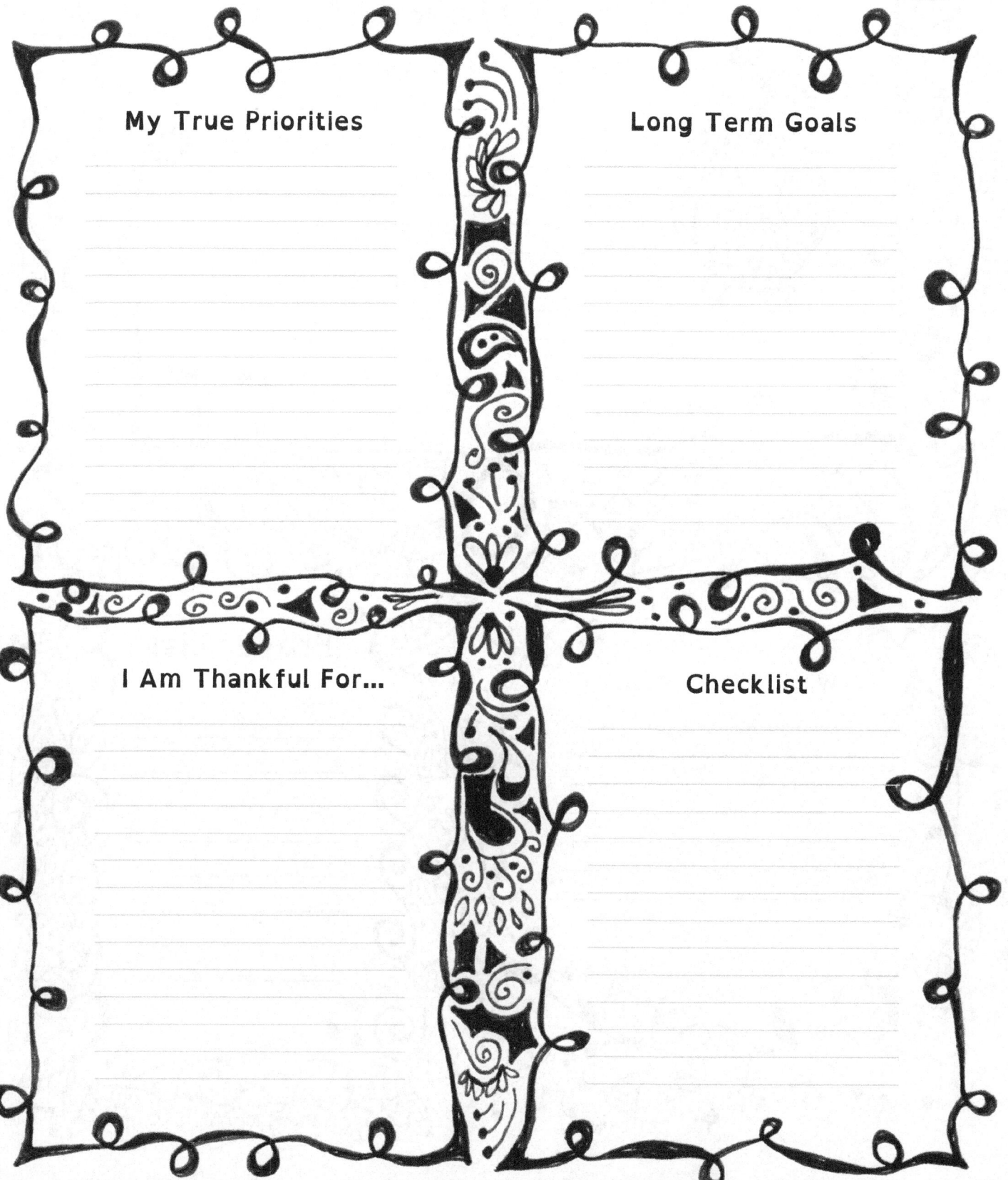

My True Priorities

Long Term Goals

I Am Thankful For...

Checklist

A New Day!

My Verse, My Song or My Prayer...

_____
_____
_____
_____
_____
_____
_____

What Matters Most...

_____
_____
_____
_____
_____

Prayer List

_____
_____
_____
_____
_____
_____
_____
_____

Mom's Coloring Time

Coloring beautiful pictures and doodling relieves stress and helps with creativity & relaxation.

"The true sign of intelligence is not knowledge but imagination." ~ Albert Einstein

Plans & Perspective

"The home is the first and most effective place to learn the lessons of life: truth, honor, virtue, self control, the value of education, honest work, and the purpose and privilege of life." - McKay

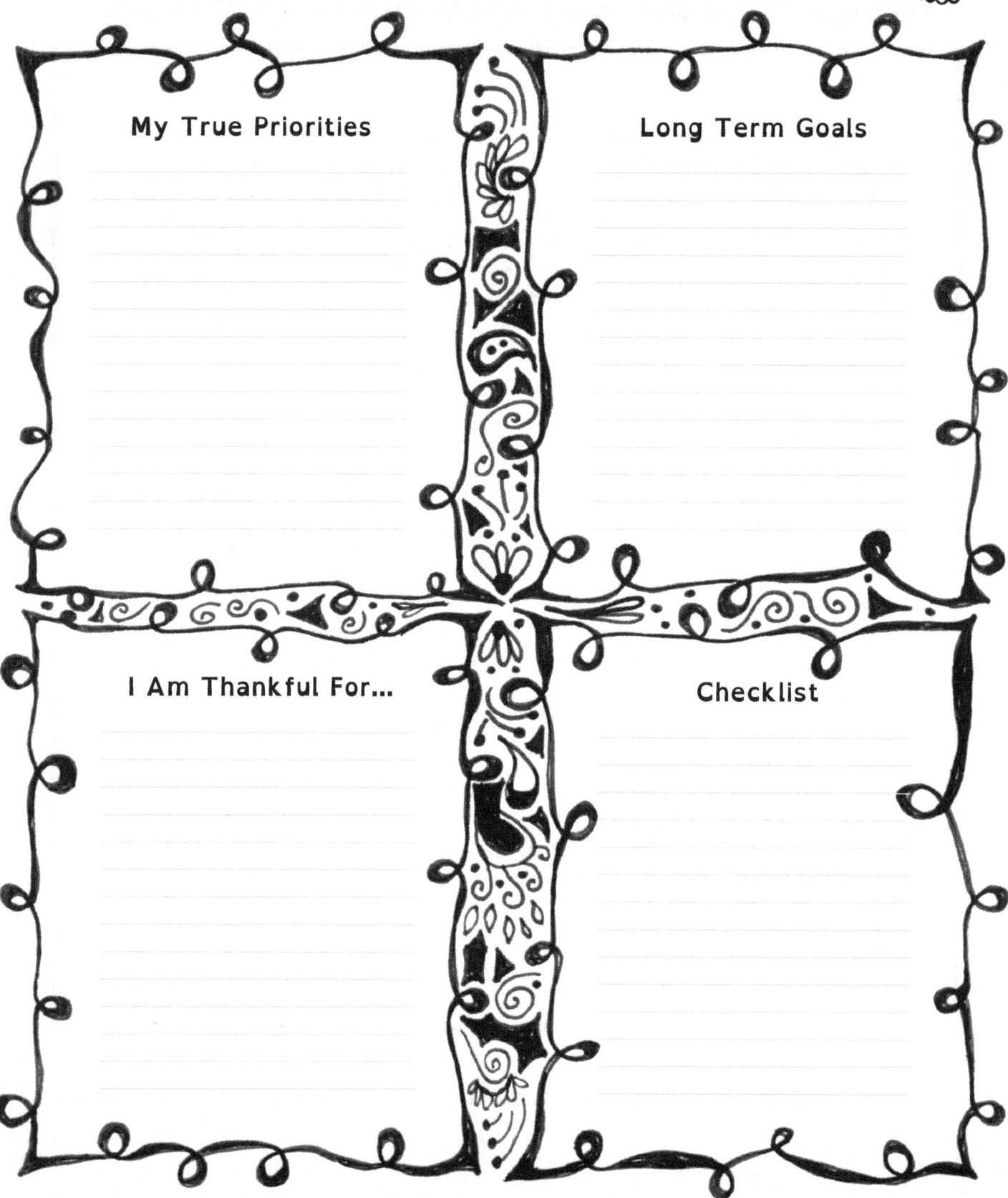

My True Priorities

Long Term Goals

I Am Thankful For...

Checklist

Attitude Improvement Time

How are your feeling today?
Color all the facial expressions that match your day!

| happy | surprised | joy | doubt | distrust |

| self-sufficiency | dreamy | shocked | scared | guile |

| gloomy | engrossment | flash | determination | thoughtful |

| diffidence | offence | confusion | craft | tired |

How is your mood influencing the people around you today?

_____

_____

Do you need a cup of tea? Some chocolate? A hug? A quiet moment? Peaceful music? Stop the clock. Make it happen. You are mom. make a little happy moment for yourself and for your family.

_____

_____

Let us not become weary in doing good, for at the proper time we will reap a harvest if we do not give up. –Galatians 6:9

Reading Time

Sit down with a few books from your stack.

Write, draw or copy the things you want to remember.

Mom's Illustrated TO-DO List

Ideas for Fun & Learning Together

Menu Planning

Open up an old-fashion cookbook!

_____
_____
_____
_____
_____

Shopping List

_____
_____
_____
_____
_____
_____
_____
_____

Draw a Meal PLAN

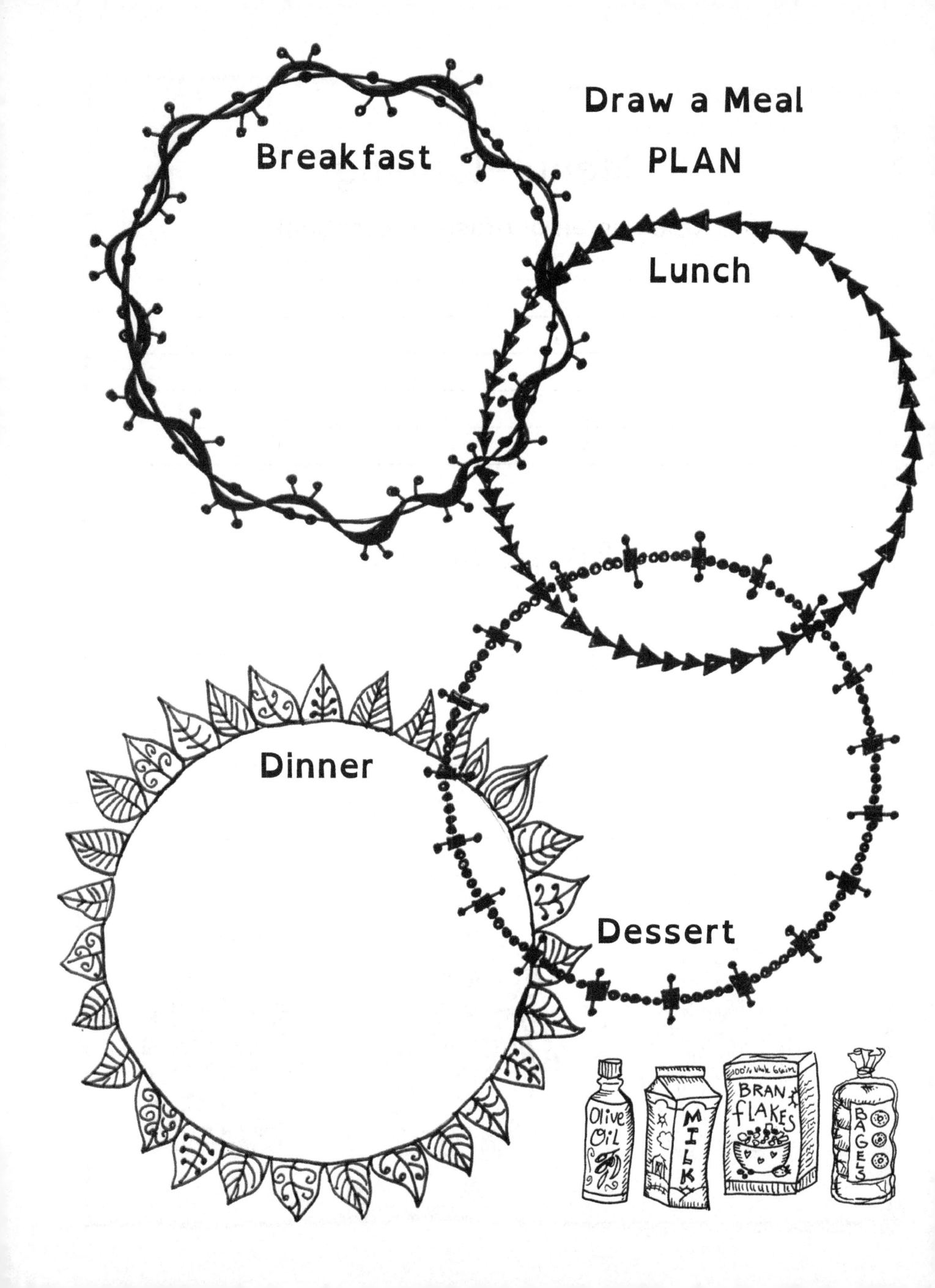

- Breakfast
- Lunch
- Dinner
- Dessert

Mom's Coloring Time

Coloring beautiful pictures and doodling relieves stress and helps with creativity & relaxation.

Recipe:

_____

Serves:

Prep Time:

Ingredients:

Instructions:

Shopping List:

"Recipe for genius: More of family and less of school, more of parents and less of peers, more creative freedom and less formal lessons." ~Raymond Moore

Mommy Math Time

Math is something that Kids need help with.
Go get a kid and show them how to do some math here:

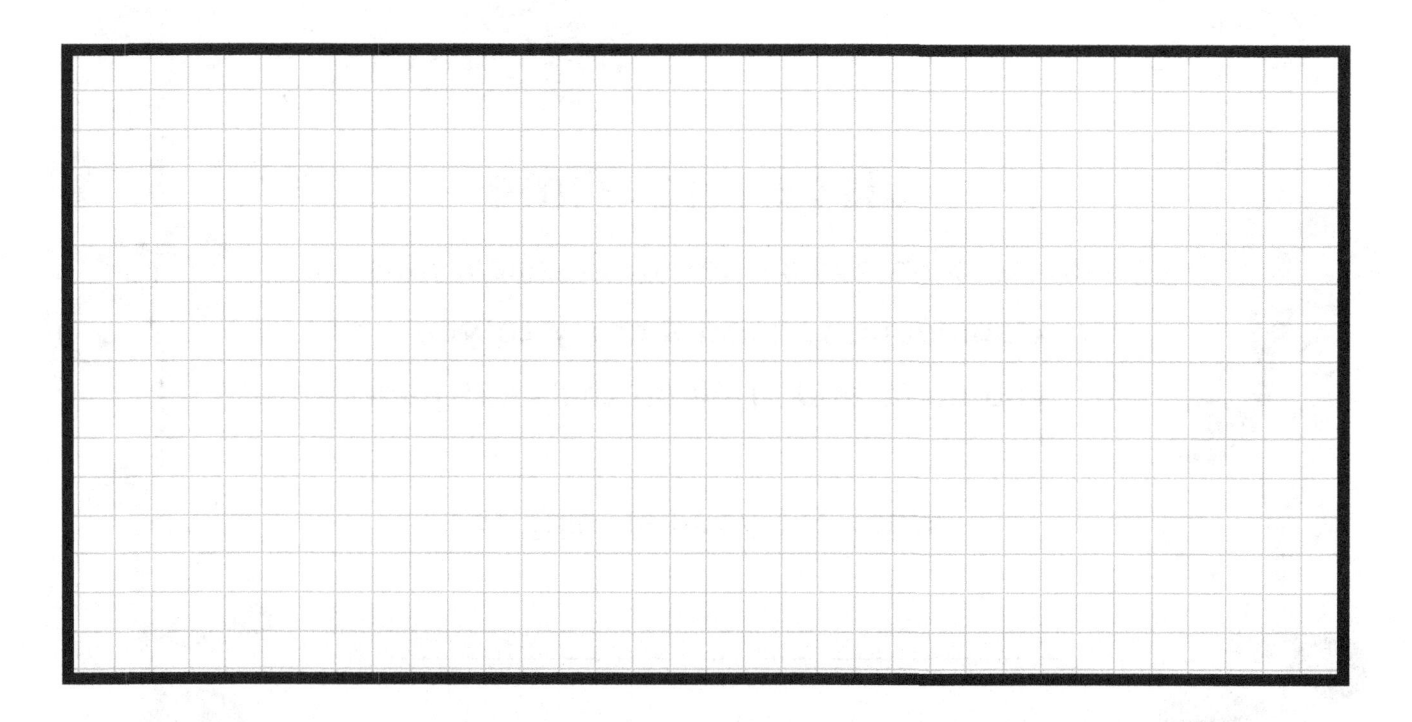

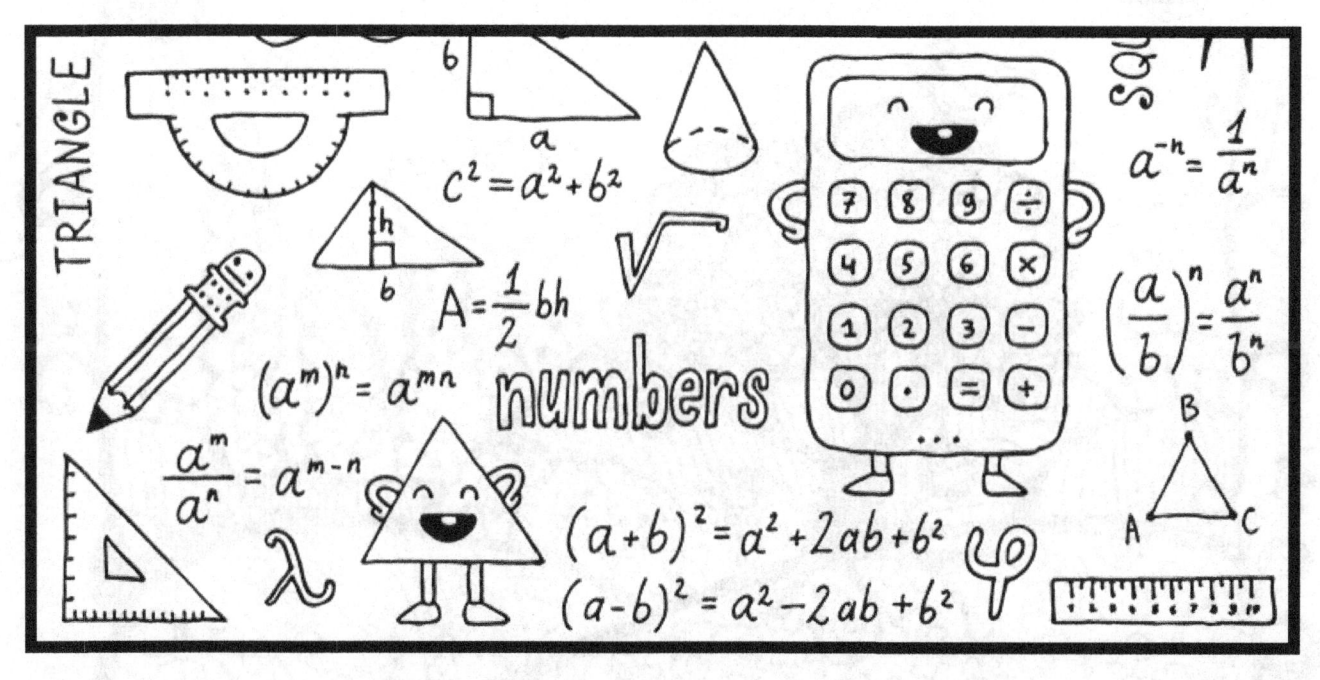

"Everything I am interested in, from cooking to electronics, is related to math. In real life you don't have to worry about integrating math into other subjects. In real life, math already is integrated into everything else." ~ Hoffstrom

Listening Time

Listen to an audio book or classical music or ask someone to read a story to you while you color and draw on the next page.

What are you listening to?

_____

Reading Time

Sit down with a few books from your stack.

Write, draw or copy the things you want to remember.

TITLE:

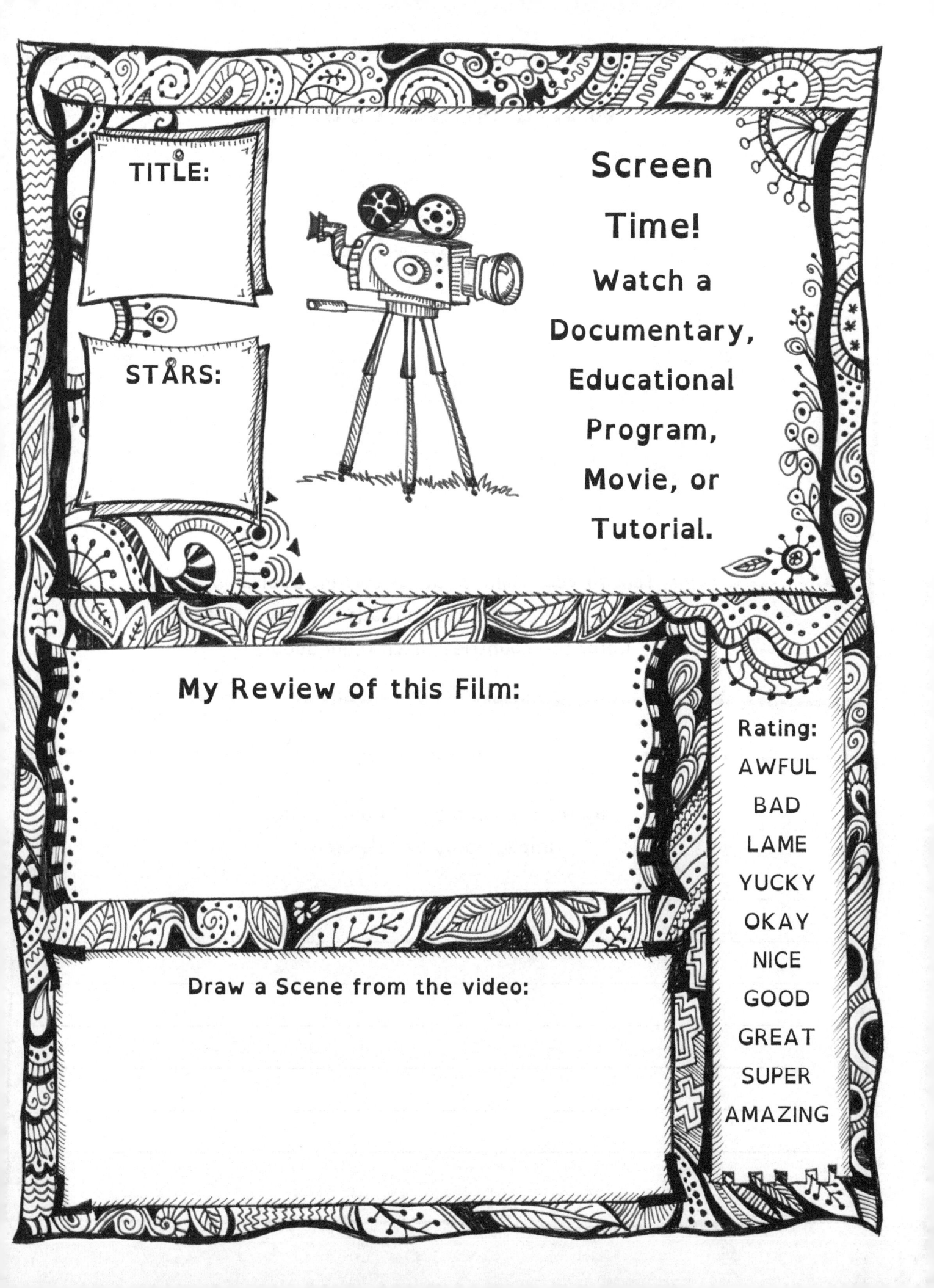

STARS:

Screen Time!

Watch a Documentary, Educational Program, Movie, or Tutorial.

My Review of this Film:

Rating:
AWFUL
BAD
LAME
YUCKY
OKAY
NICE
GOOD
GREAT
SUPER
AMAZING

Draw a Scene from the video:

World News Today!

Talk to your children about current events.
Look at a newspaper, news broadcast or website.
Color the countries teach them about.

Pray for the People and Communities
impacted by Bad News:

_____
_____
_____
_____
_____
_____
_____

Daily Journal

_____
_____
_____
_____
_____
_____
_____
_____
_____
_____

"Education is not filling a bucket,
but lighting a fire." ~W.B. Yeats

Special Memories
Things that you want to remember...

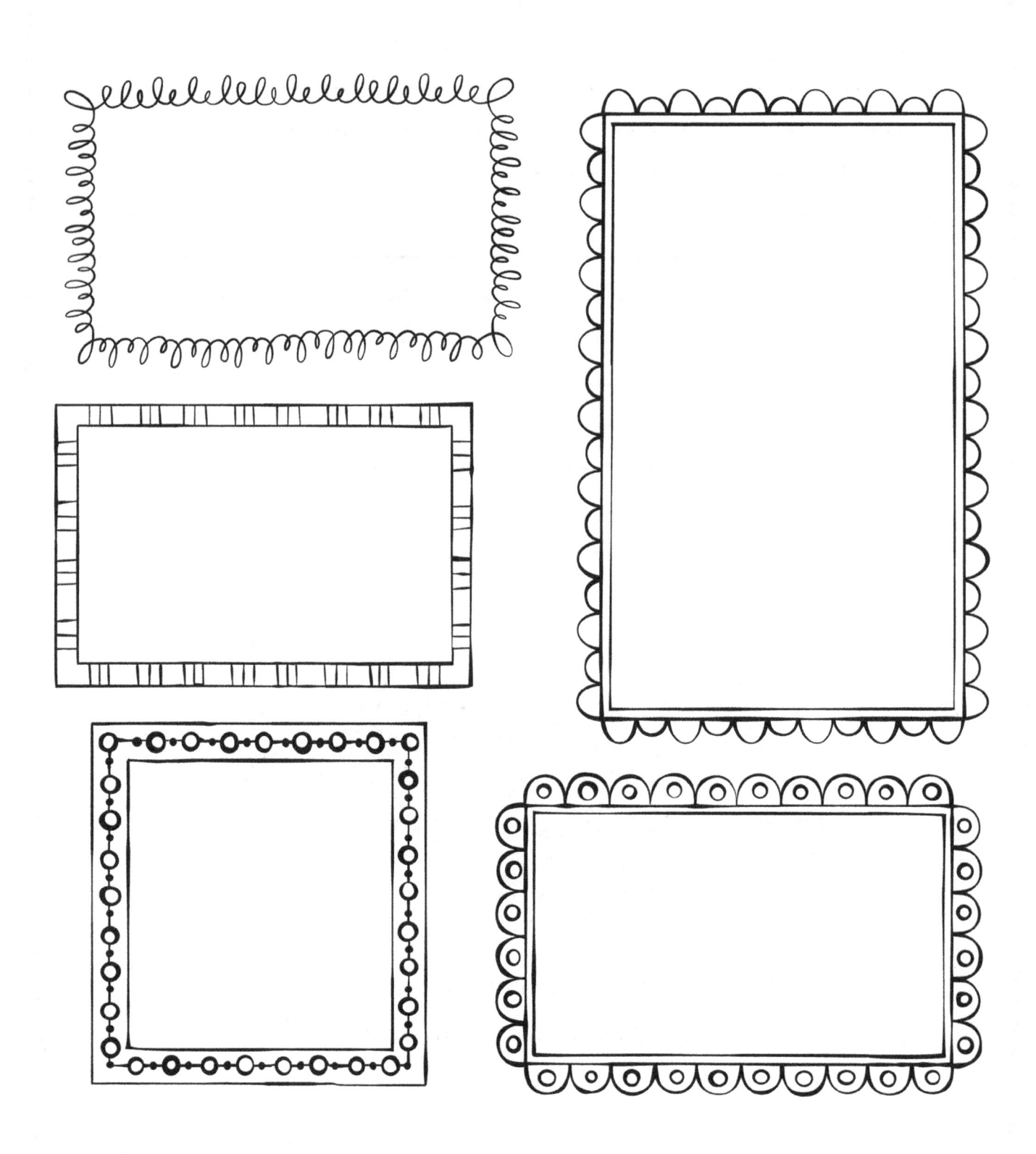

A New Day!

My Verse, My Song or My Prayer...

What Matters Most...

Prayer List

Mom's Coloring Time

Coloring beautiful pictures and doodling relieves stress and helps with creativity & relaxation.

"The true sign of intelligence is not knowledge but imagination." ~ Albert Einstein

Plans & Perspective

"The home is the first and most effective place to learn the lessons of life: truth, honor, virtue, self control, the value of education, honest work, and the purpose and privilege of life." - McKay

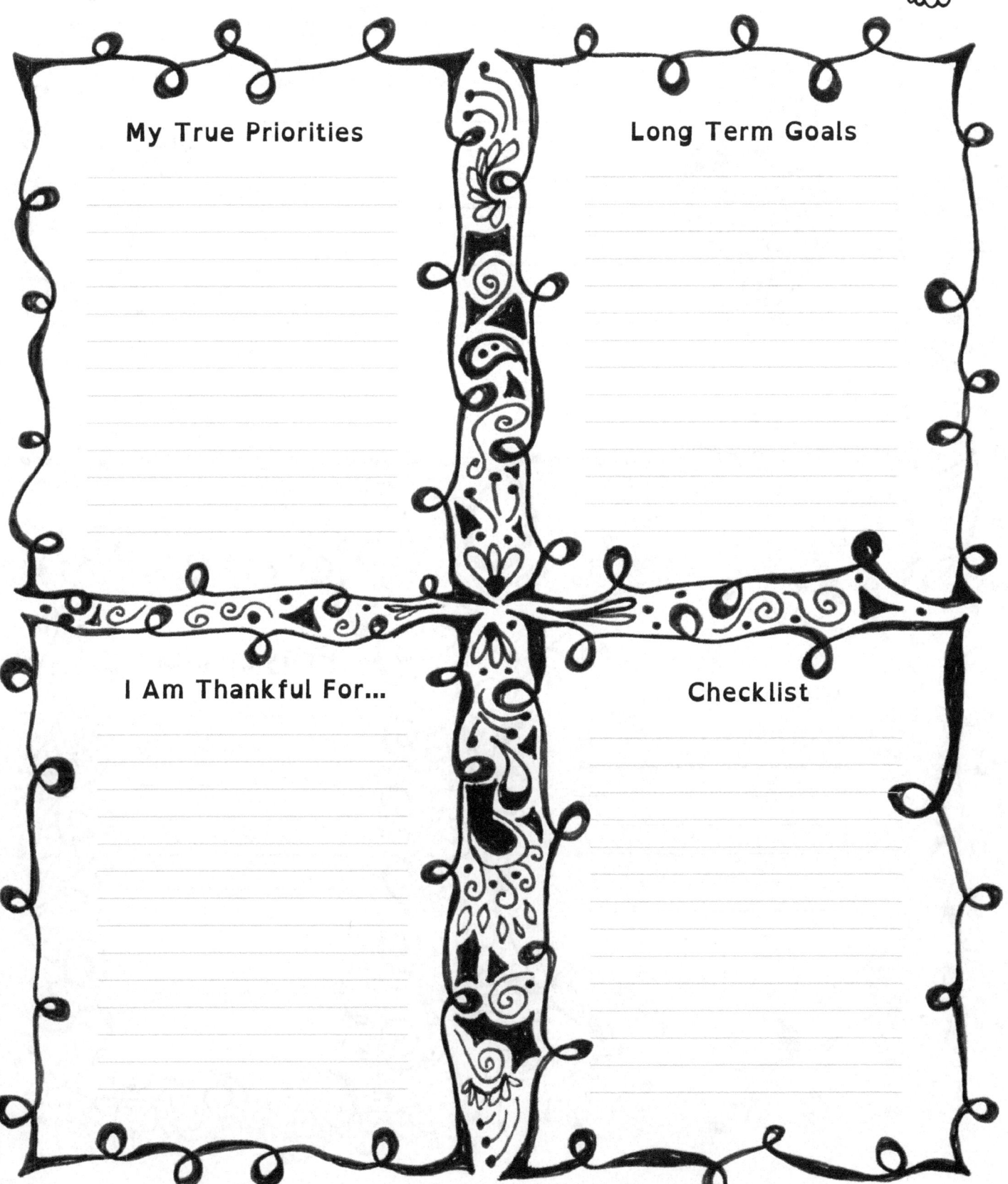

My True Priorities

Long Term Goals

I Am Thankful For...

Checklist

A New Day!

My Verse, My Song or My Prayer...

What Matters Most...

Prayer List

Mom's Coloring Time

Coloring beautiful pictures and doodling relieves stress and helps with creativity & relaxation.

"The true sign of intelligence is not knowledge but imagination." ~ Albert Einstein

Plans & Perspective

"The home is the first and most effective place to learn the lessons of life: truth, honor, virtue, self control, the value of education, honest work, and the purpose and privilege of life." - McKay

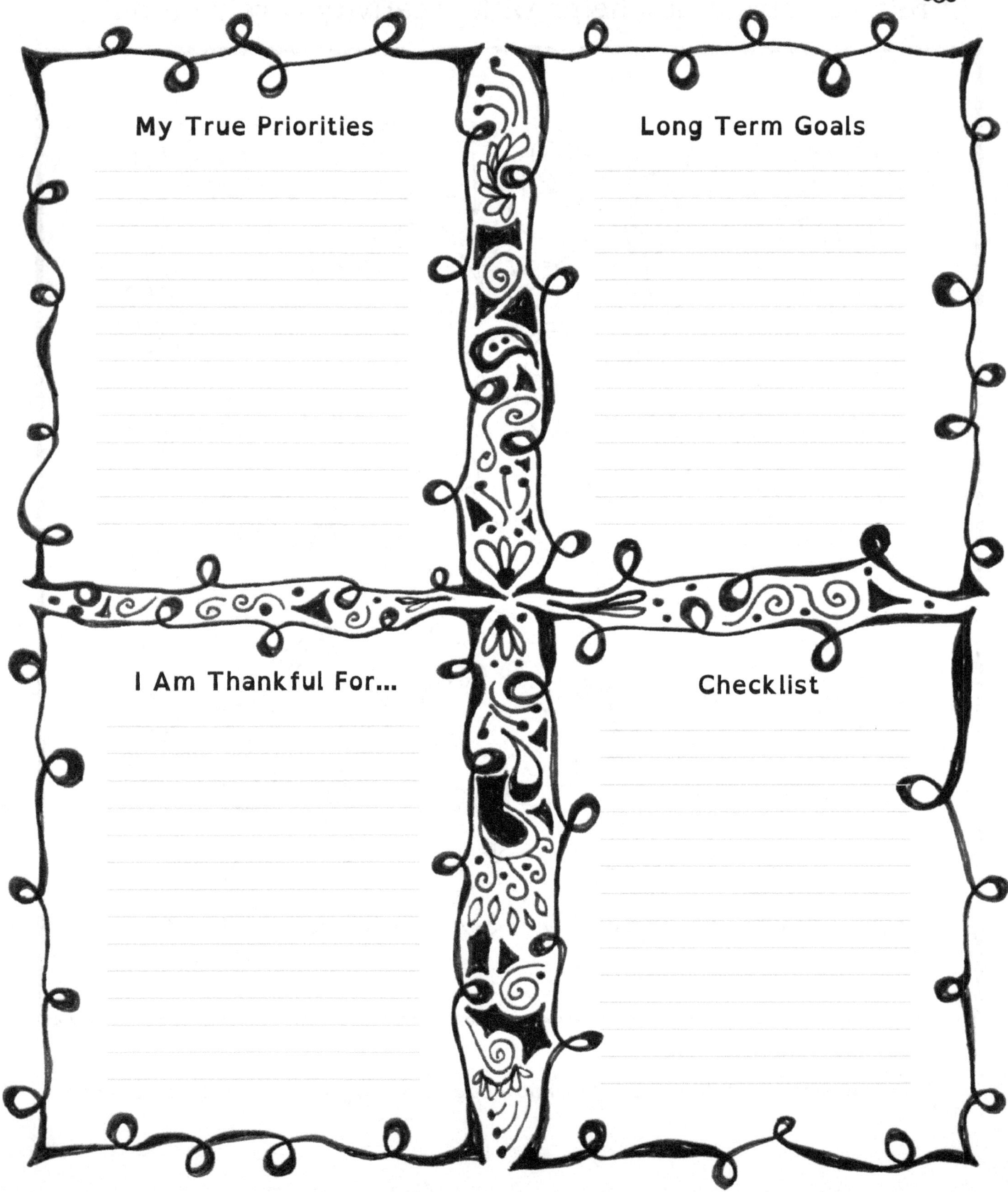

My True Priorities

Long Term Goals

I Am Thankful For...

Checklist

Attitude Improvement Time

How are your feeling today?
Color all the facial expressions that match your day!

happy	surprised	joy	doubt	distrust
self-sufficiency	dreamy	shocked	scared	guile
gloomy	engrossment	flash	determination	thoughtful
diffidence	offence	confusion	craft	tired

How is your mood influencing the people around you today?

___

___

Do you need a cup of tea? Some chocolate? A hug? A quiet moment? Peaceful music? Stop the clock. Make it happen. You are mom. make a little happy moment for yourself and for your family.

___

___

Let us not become weary in doing good, for at the proper time we will reap a harvest if we do not give up. –Galatians 6:9

Reading Time

Sit down with a few books from your stack.

Write, draw or copy the things you want to remember.

Mom's Illustrated TO-DO List

Ideas for Fun & Learning Together

Menu Planning

Open up an old-fashion cookbook!

_____
_____
_____
_____
_____
_____

Shopping List

_____
_____
_____
_____
_____
_____
_____
_____
_____

Draw a Meal PLAN

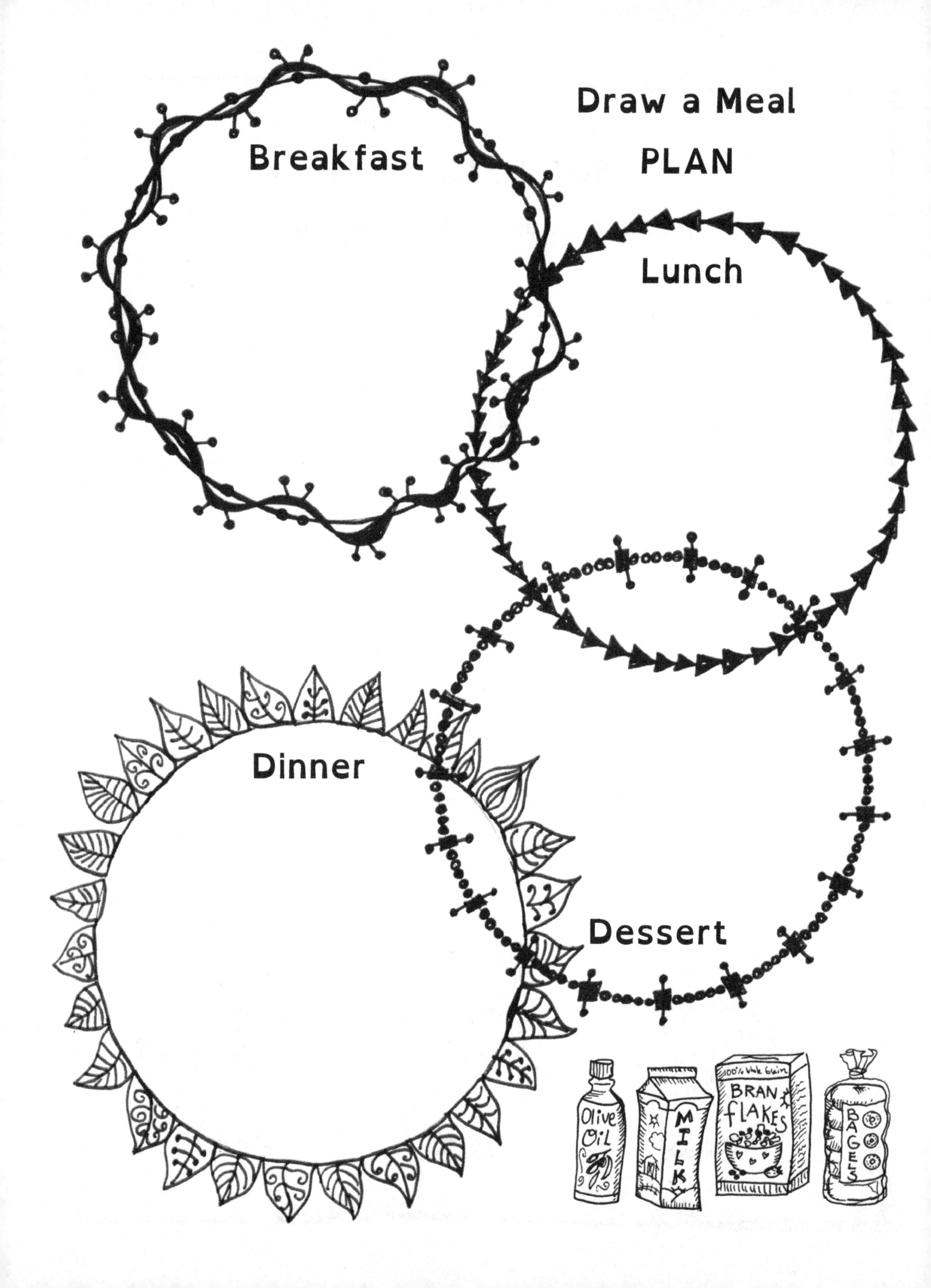

- Breakfast
- Lunch
- Dinner
- Dessert

Recipe:

_____

Serves:

Prep Time:

Ingredients:

Instructions:

Shopping List:

"Recipe for genius: More of family and less of school, more of parents and less of peers, more creative freedom and less formal lessons." ~Raymond Moore

Mommy Math Time

Math is something that Kids need help with.
Go get a kid and show them how to do some math here:

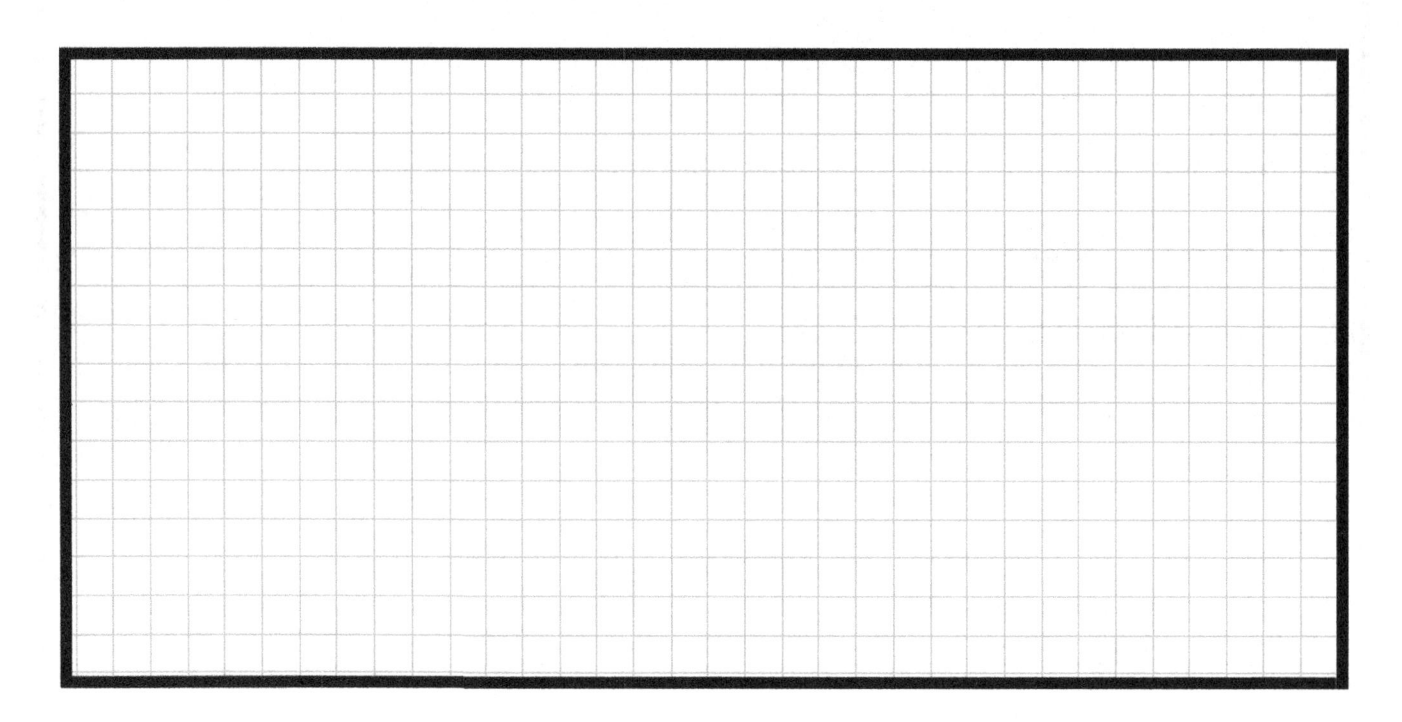

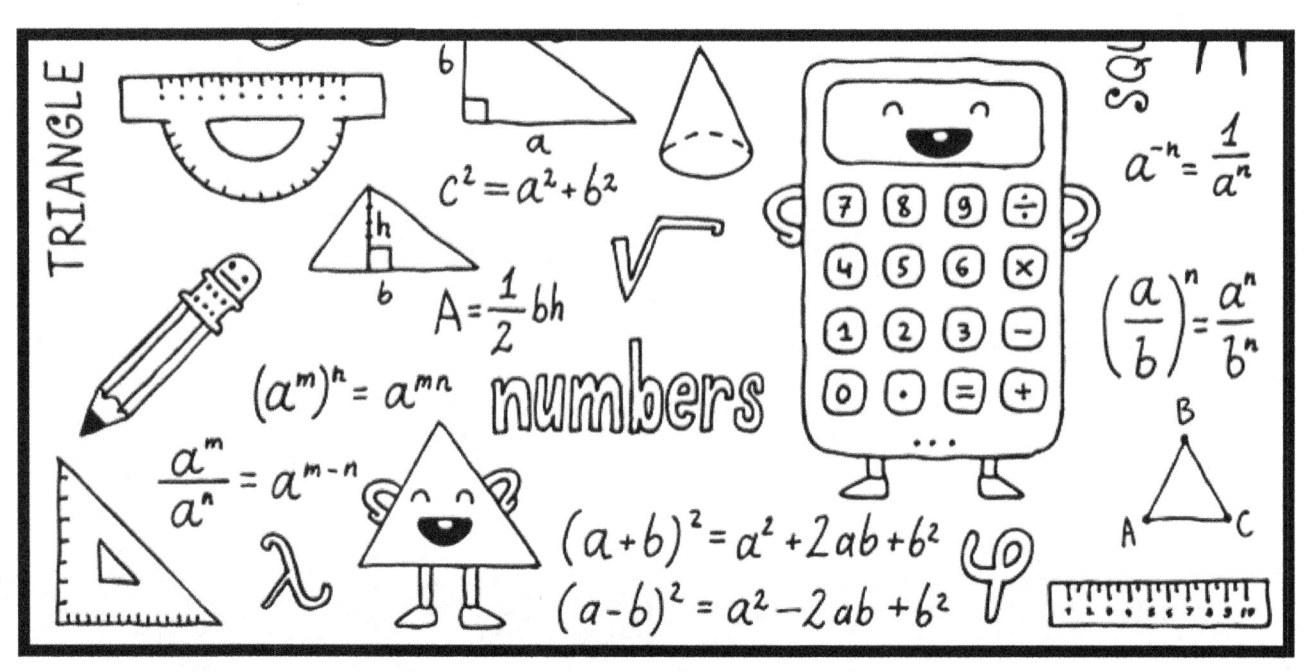

"Everything I am interested in, from cooking to electronics, is related to math. In real life you don't have to worry about integrating math into other subjects. In real life, math already is integrated into everything else." ~ Hoffstrom

Listening Time

Listen to an audio book or classical music or ask someone to read a story to you while you color and draw on the next page.

What are you listening to?

_____

Reading Time

Sit down with a few books from your stack.

Write, draw or copy the things you want to remember.

TITLE:

STARS:

Screen Time!

Watch a Documentary, Educational Program, Movie, or Tutorial.

My Review of this Film:

Draw a Scene from the video:

Rating:
AWFUL
BAD
LAME
YUCKY
OKAY
NICE
GOOD
GREAT
SUPER
AMAZING

World News Today!

Talk to your children about current events.
Look at a newspaper, news broadcast or website.
Color the countries teach them about.

Pray for the People and Communities
impacted by Bad News:

_____
_____
_____
_____
_____
_____
_____

Daily Journal

_____
_____
_____
_____
_____
_____
_____
_____
_____
_____

"Education is not filling a bucket,
but lighting a fire." ~W.B. Yeats

Special Memories
Things that you want to remember...

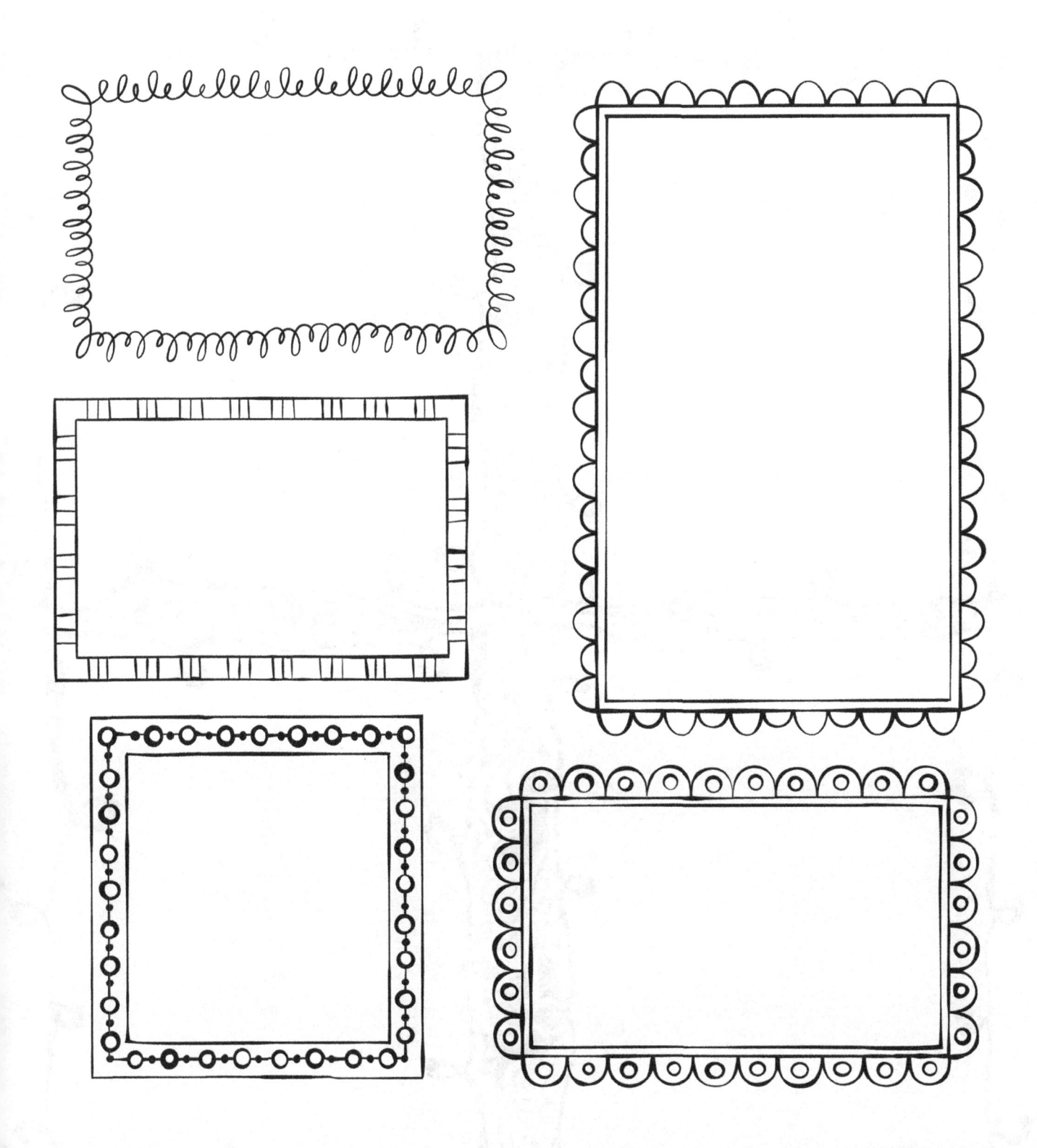

Reading Time

Sit down with a few books from your stack.

Write, draw or copy the things you want to remember.

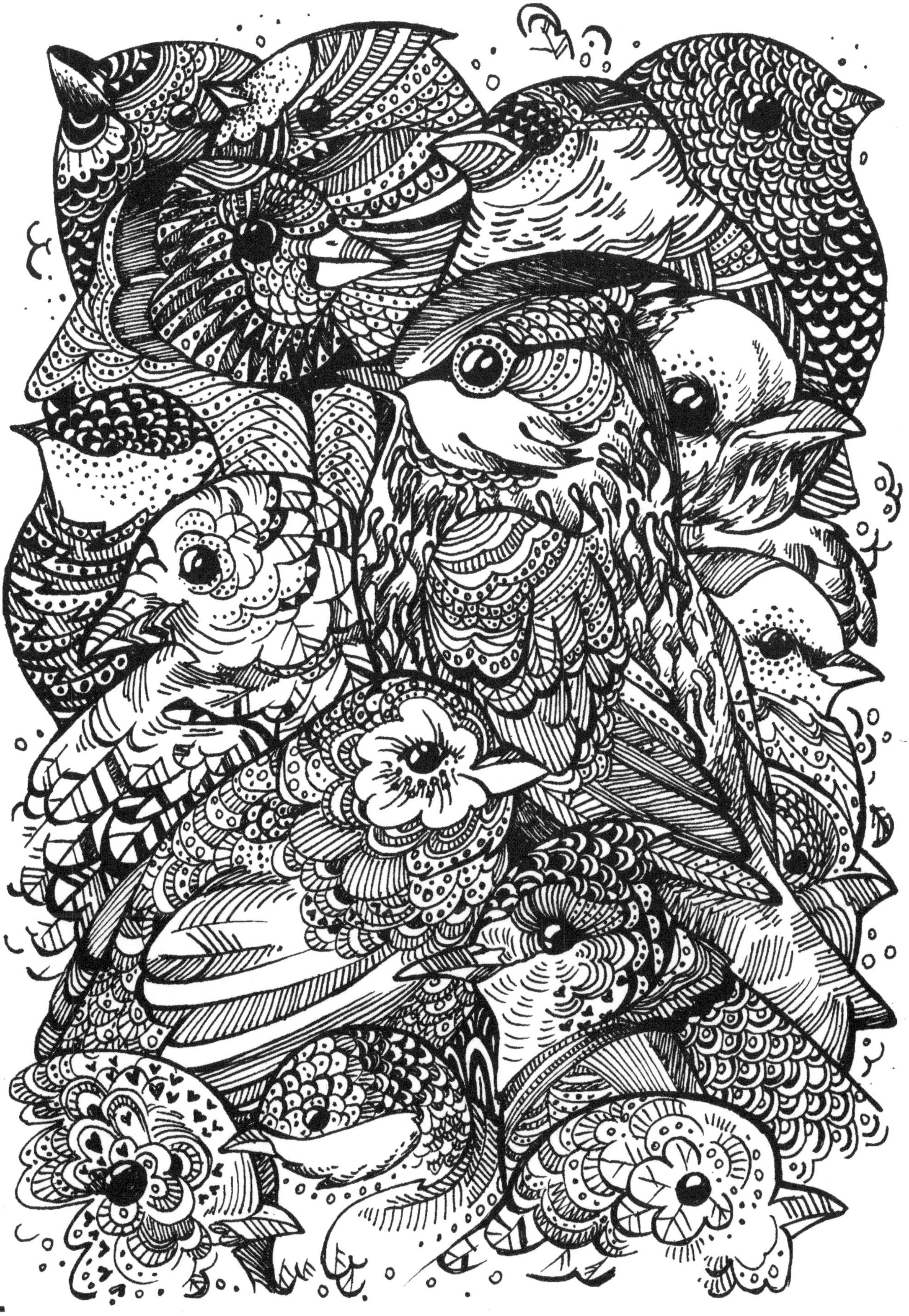

Made in United States
Orlando, FL
17 May 2024